PROFESSIONAL DIALOGUES IN THE EARLY YEARS

Rediscovering early years pedagogy and principles

Critical Guides for Teacher Educators

You might also like the following books in this series from Critical Publishing.

Ability Grouping in Primary Schools: Case Studies and Critical Debates
Rachel Marks
978-1-910391-24-2

Beginning Teachers' Learning: Making Experience Count
Burn, Hagger and Mutton
978-1-910391-17-4

Coteaching in Teacher Education: Innovative Pedagogy for Excellence
Colette Murphy
978-1-910391-82-2

Developing Creative and Critical Educational Practitioners
Victoria Door
978-1-909682-37-5

Developing Outstanding Practice in School-based Teacher Education
Edited by Kim Jones and Elizabeth White
978-1-909682-41-2

Evidence-based Teaching in Primary Education
Edited by Val Poultney
978-1-911196-46-3

Tackling Social Disadvantage through Teacher Education
Ian Thompson
978-1-912096-61-9

Teacher Education Partnerships: Policy and Practice
Mutton, Burn, Hagger, and Thirlwall
978-1-912096-57-2

Teacher Educators in the Twenty-first Century: Identity, Knowledge and Research
Gerry Czerniawski
978-1-912096-53-4

Teacher Status and Professional Learning: The Place Model
Linda Clarke
978-1-910391-46-4

Theories of Professional Learning
Carey Philpott
978-1-909682-33-7

Our titles are also available in a range of electronic formats. To order please go to our website www.criticalpublishing.com or contact our distributor NBN International by telephoning 01752 202301 or emailing orders@nbninternational.com.

PROFESSIONAL DIALOGUES IN THE EARLY YEARS

Rediscovering early years pedagogy and principles

Series Editor: Ian Menter

Critical Guides for Teacher Educators

CRITICAL PUBLISHING

Mary Wild
Elise Alexander
Mary Briggs
Catharine Gilson
Gillian Lake
Helena Mitchell
Nick Swarbrick

First published in 2018 by Critical Publishing Ltd

All rights reserved. No part of this publication may be reproduced, stored in a retrieval system, or transmitted in any form or by any means, electronic, mechanical, photocopying, recording or otherwise, without prior permission in writing from the publisher.

The authors have made every effort to ensure the accuracy of information contained in this publication, but assume no responsibility for any errors, inaccuracies, inconsistencies and omissions. Likewise every effort has been made to contact copyright holders. If any copyright material has been reproduced unwittingly and without permission the publisher will gladly receive information enabling them to rectify any error or omission in subsequent editions.

Copyright © (2018) Elise Alexander, Mary Briggs, Catharine Gilson, Gillian Lake, Helena Mitchell, Nick Swarbrick and Mary Wild

British Library Cataloguing in Publication Data
A CIP record for this book is available from the British Library

ISBN: 9781912508242

This book is also available in the following e-book formats:
MOBI: 9781912508259
EPUB: 9781912508266
Adobe e-book reader: 9781912508273

The rights of Elise Alexander, Mary Briggs, Catharine Gilson, Gillian Lake, Helena Mitchell, Nick Swarbrick and Mary Wild to be identified as the Authors of this work has been asserted by them in accordance with the Copyright, Design and Patents Act 1988.

Cover and text design by Greensplash Limited
Project Management by Out of House Publishing
Printed and bound in Great Britain by 4edge, Essex

Critical Publishing
3 Connaught Road
St Albans
AL3 5RX

www.criticalpublishing.com

Paper from responsible sources

CONTENTS

	Foreword	*vii*
	About the editors and authors	*viii*
Chapter 1	Introduction: current contexts for professional development in early years education *Mary Wild*	1
Chapter 2	What does professional dialogue mean? *Elise Alexander*	13
Chapter 3	Revisiting values and ethical standpoints in early years education *Helena Mitchell and Nick Swarbrick*	25
Chapter 4	The learning relationship: principles of effective learning and practice in the early years *Gillian Lake*	38
Chapter 5	Understanding the family and cultural contexts for learning *Catharine Gilson*	53
Chapter 6	The informed practitioner *Mary Briggs*	65
	References	*81*
	Index	*88*

FOREWORD

Historically, the early years sector of educational provision has been characterised by an enormous paradox. It is the sector where all the foundations of learning are laid and has been consistently demonstrated to have great significance for later educational success (Sylva et al, 2010). Yet at the same time it has often been undervalued and treated as less demanding for the staff who work in this sector rather than in other parts of the education system (Moyles, 2001). That this paradox persists into the twenty-first century is both disconcerting and alarming. The best early years practice, whether it be in schools, day nurseries or elsewhere, is only achieved through the development of considerable skill and knowledge by those who practise therein, whether they be teachers, early years practitioners or classroom assistants.

It is therefore a great pleasure to welcome this new volume into the series of *Critical Guides for Teacher Educators*. Mary Wild and her colleagues at Oxford Brookes University offer us a collection of invaluable insights into the challenges faced by early years practitioners and offer many suggestions about how those who are educating those practitioners may encourage the development of the qualities required. This collection is imbued with a deep sense of the ethical, social and emotional responsibilities of early years practitioners, as well as the very real cognitive demands that working in this sector produces. It also recognises the importance of interprofessional collaboration in this sector and the crucial importance of effective communication with children's parents and carers.

In short, this book – *Professional dialogues in the early years: Re-discovering early years pedagogy and principles* offers a redress to those who undervalue the sector and will be of immense value to those who have responsibility for cultivating future generations of high-quality staff to work with the youngest children.

Ian Menter, Series Editor
Emeritus Professor of Teacher Education, University of Oxford

ABOUT THE EDITORS AND AUTHORS

ABOUT THE SERIES EDITOR

Ian Menter is Emeritus Professor of Teacher Education and was formerly the director of Professional Programmes in the department of education at the University of Oxford. He previously worked at the Universities of Glasgow, the West of Scotland, London Metropolitan, the West of England and Gloucestershire. Before that he was a primary school teacher in Bristol, England. His most recent publications include *A Companion to Research in Teacher Education* (edited with Michael Peters and Bronwen Cowie) and *Learning to Teach in England and the United States* (Tatto, Burn, Menter, Mutton and Thompson). His work has also been published in many academic journals.

ABOUT THE BOOK EDITOR

Mary Wild is Head of the School of Education at Oxford Brookes University, having previously been principal lecturer (student experience), senior lecturer in child development and education, and subject coordinator for early childhood studies. Her research interests include early childhood literacy, children's thinking and the use of information and communication technology (ICT) to support learning. She has taught across a range of courses for practitioners and professionals in early years and is a qualified teacher with experience in both the primary and early years sectors. She is a member of the National Strategy Group for the Early Childhood Studies Degree Network and of the Strategic Schools Partnership Board for Oxfordshire. Mary is a member of the British Psychological Society, the British Educational Research Association and Universities Council for the Education of Teachers (UCET).

ABOUT THE AUTHORS

Elise Alexander is a senior lecturer in early childhood studies at Oxford Brookes University and is currently subject coordinator for the Early Childhood Studies (ECS) programme. She is engaged in researching the experience of early years students in higher education and has an interest in the development of professional identity in ECS students and in higher education pedagogy. In her previous role as principal lecturer in early childhood studies at University of Roehampton she carried out an Economic and Social Research Council (ESRC)-funded project that investigated practitioners' understanding of quality in their work with children. She is a member of TACTYC and regularly attends meeting of the Early Childhood Studies Degrees Network.

Mary Briggs is a principal lecturer and programme lead for primary and early years initial teacher education (ITE) at Oxford Brookes University. She is a Fellow of the Royal Society of Arts and a Chartered Teacher of Mathematics. She teaches on a wide range of different education courses and has published widely in the educational field. Her specific research interests are in mathematics education, leadership, assessment and mentoring and coaching. She has worked in a wide range of settings including children's homes, special schools, primary school and universities.

Catharine Gilson is a senior lecturer in early childhood education at Oxford Brookes University. She has experience of teaching across a range of courses including the early years strand of the Postgraduate Course in Education (PGCE) and the early childhood studies degree. She has previously worked as a teacher and as a local authority early years advisory teacher. Her doctorate focused on the learning and teaching relationship between adults and three- to five-year-old children and other research interests include children's rights and children's voice and observational methods.

Gillian Lake was a primary teacher in Ireland for many years before first undertaking an MSc in child development and education, and then being awarded the Talbot Scholarship to read a doctorate of philosophy in education at the University of Oxford, focusing on the early years. Her research comprised the design, development and evaluation of an oral language intervention targeting vocabulary and narrative development of children aged three to four years. The results have been promising and she hopes to further investigate the possibility of introducing this intervention as a professional development tool for early years practitioners. She has an ongoing research interest in early childhood education, oral language interventions, narrative development, pretend play and emerging literacy.

Helena Mitchell is currently a visiting fellow at Oxford Brookes University. She is Vice Chair (Research and Knowledge Exchange) and treasurer for the Early Childhood Studies Degrees Network, a voluntary organisation that brings together institutions across the UK which run degrees in early childhood studies. Prior to taking on this role she was Head of the School of Education at Oxford Brookes University. She led the primary Postgraduate Course in Education (PGCE) programme and also the early childhood studies degree when it was introduced at Oxford Brookes in 2000. She has extensive experience as a classroom teacher. She is a member of British Education Research Association (BERA), TACTYC and the Society for Research into Higher Education (SRHE), and a trustee of Peeple, a charity that supports parents and children learning together. Her most recent research has focused on graduates from early childhood studies degrees and their transition to professional status as teachers and leaders in early years settings. She is also currently involved in a research project on values and beliefs in primary education, a collaborative partnership with primary teachers.

Nick Swarbrick is programme lead for the undergraduate degrees in the school of education, teaching on the undergraduate degree in early childhood studies and the primary Postgraduate Course in Education (PGCE), principally around early years pedagogy. He has a research and teaching role in children's literature and how young children explore the outdoors environment. Nick holds an associate teaching fellowship at the university and is a senior fellow of the Higher Education Academy. Prior to joining Oxford Brookes he was headteacher of a multi-cultural nursery school in Oxford city, which pioneered the Forest School project in Oxfordshire and supported a school-based Initial Teacher Training Scheme.

CHAPTER 1 | INTRODUCTION: CURRENT CONTEXTS FOR PROFESSIONAL DEVELOPMENT IN EARLY YEARS EDUCATION

Mary Wild

CRITICAL ISSUES

- What are the issues and challenges facing educators* in working with students* in the early years sector?
- How can educators support their students in a way that recognises and is responsive to the voice and needs of the students?
- Why is it important to emphasise critical reflection and professional dialogue based on principles and values rather than competences in early years education?

*Definitions: The terminology used to denote roles within the early years sector range widely and this is replicated in the diverse terminology that can be applied to those who contribute to their professional development. For the sake of simplicity this book will adopt the term 'educators' to refer to those who provide training and professional development and 'students' and sometimes 'professionals' to refer those who are being supported through training or professional development.

Introduction

In order to provide nurturing and enabling environments for young children to learn and flourish emotionally and socially as well as cognitively, it is imperative that teachers and practitioners make well-informed and thoughtful decisions about the experiences they provide for the children in their care. There is no shortage of texts that steer or guide professionals working in the early years towards acquiring particular skills and competencies or particular pedagogic approaches but there are fewer texts that seek to open up debates about the underlying assumptions and evidence base to inform practice. There are even fewer texts that are addressed primarily towards educators who are responsible for guiding and supporting students across what has become an increasingly complicated and often fast-changing backdrop of policy and provision for the training of those already working in the early years sector as well as those seeking to join the sector's workforce.

The purpose of this book is to provide educators for the early years sector with a starting point for supporting students that is not driven by the most recent set of approved standards and competences but rests, more surely perhaps, upon a set of fundamental principles and philosophies for early years pedagogy and that fosters critical reflection and professional dialogue on the nature of early years education. The book will be framed by a principle of continued professional dialogue as integral to, and essential for, effective practice. In order to have professional dialogue professionals need to have an informed and principled knowledge base to draw upon and the critical skills to interrogate and evaluate these sources of knowledge. This book will also take an ethical standpoint that considers the child to be an active agent in their own learning, whose views and opinions as well as fundamental needs must be the cornerstone of education in the early years. This principle will be extrapolated to the students with whom teacher educators work, whose voice and agency in their own development should be similarly respected and reflected, which is not to say that as educators we should never challenge our students' views. This book will provide early years teacher educators with critical guidance to explore enduring philosophies and principles of early years pedagogy and to creatively interpret and communicate these to those they are training to be teachers and professionals in these crucial early years of children's development and education.

In this opening chapter some of the current context for professional development in early education is outlined but the emphasis is less on specific policy initiatives, which may always be subject to change but on some rather more deep-seated trends and issues that challenge those working to educate others within the sector and which highlight some perennial tensions in developing the professional profile of the sector as well as the professional identities of those within it.

A context of change

Over the past two decades the early years sector has experienced an unprecedented degree of focus and attention from policy-makers of all political persuasions, both nationally and internationally. This attention has included a foregrounding of professional training and qualifications across the sector. These developments are charted in a joint review of early years research published by British Education Research Association (BERA) and TACTYC in 2017, which is highlighted in the recommended reading to be found at the end of this chapter (BERA/TACTYC, 2017). One of the most recent qualifications introduced in England is the Early Years Teacher (EYT) status and the antecedents of this initiative are captured in a paper by Henshall et al (2018), which also provides a useful review of the development of early years qualifications in England. This drive towards a greater level of workforce qualifications in the early years is repeated elsewhere in the world and a number of studies located in other countries are also included as recommended reading. However, it is not the intention to review these policy developments in depth in this chapter, partly because they are already so expertly summarised (BERA/TACTYC, 2017, Henshall et al, 2018) but more importantly because this book is intended to support educators in a manner that can maintain the focus on principles and understanding that are relevant irrespective of particular policy initiatives or qualifications that can readily be altered by a change of government or at the instigation of regulatory authorities.

Of course it would be foolish to pretend that our work as educators exists in a policy vacuum and so although specific policies and qualifications will not be singled out it is important to draw attention to some underlying trends and challenges that are apparent in policy-making and pertinent to the ways in which we educate students and professionals in the early years. These include a series of contentious issues such as what constitutes quality in early years and how it is seen to drive policy, a trend towards school readiness as a principal aim of early years education and associated debates about the relative balance to be struck between education and care imperatives in working with our youngest children. We shall return to these debates that have intensified in recent decades but first let us consider some more enduring characteristics of the early years workforce.

Continuities in professional contexts

Despite the policy imperative towards a more qualified workforce in early years there remain some persistent features of the early years workforce that will impact the ways in which educators are able to work. In an article examining the distinction between '*being a professional*' as opposed to '*practising professionally*' Dyer (2018) highlights figures from the Department for Education (DfE, 2017), which show that over 80 per cent of early years provision remains in the private, voluntary and independent (PVI) sector. This means that substantial variations remain in regard to the terms and conditions of employees within the early years (EY) sector and this variation extends even in regard to their job titles and roles, both as described and as experienced, in different parts of the sector. Notwithstanding an increase in the number of graduate courses in the sector and of those holding qualifications with nominally equivalent status to qualified teacher status (QTS), the general level of societal status as well as terms and conditions remain relatively low. Furthermore, there is no '*clear, nationally agreed career progression or professional infrastructure to ensure the collective voice of practitioners*' (Dyer, 2018, p 349). Thus it can be argued that a traditional marker of a professional workforce, which is to be a collective body with clear and publicly recognised parameters of experience and status, does not pertain in the same way as it would do for teachers in other phases in education. In the empirical element of her research project working with students on a BA Early Years undergraduate course, Dyer further highlights the differential career trajectories and aspirations of these students and for some of them the anomalies and challenges they face in studying for higher level qualifications when they return to a workplace setting where they may then be more qualified than their senior managers.

The diverse nature of settings and workplace contexts coupled with the broad spectrum of workplace needs mean that as an educator supporting professional development within the early years sector you may frequently encounter both a varied array of courses to work on and professionally diverse cohorts to work with. Even within cohorts there is likely to be considerable variation in the contexts and settings from which your students have come.

Reflection

For example, you might be teaching a seemingly clearly delineated course such as an Early Childhood Studies degree course that is aligned to well-defined benchmarks (QAA, 2014). However, within the group you have students who have arrived on the course straight from school, with relatively little voluntary experience of working with children, alongside some who have studied a more vocational childcare qualification at an Further Education (FE) college. Before you there is also a small group of more mature students who have returned to study after having their own families and are now wishing to retrain and a further group of experienced practitioners who are completing a top-up qualification, having successfully completed a Foundation degree at an FE college. Some, but not all, of this cohort are aiming to complete the EYT course alongside their degree studies.

» How will you pitch your intended teaching to accommodate the range of experience and perspectives in the group?

» How will you ensure active engagement and mutual respect for differing perspectives and degrees of experience?

» What will be the key personal and communication skills you will need to utilise in this situation?

A gendered workforce

One of the persistent features of the early years workforce is the under-representation of male students and employees. As Brownhill and Oates (2016) note in their study of gender perceptions and roles in the early years sector, 98 per cent of the 0–5 years workforce is female. They offer a fascinating insight into some of the ramifications of this imbalance in which both genders are presumed to exhibit different characteristics and strengths and have stereotypical roles imposed upon them. Men working in the early years can feel especially pressurised to serve as male role models. As an educator it is worth reflecting on how you will incorporate gender-sensitive reflection into your tutoring whilst ensuring against tokenism or all too easy stereotyping.

Knowing our students and avoiding assumptions

One of the growing trends in research on early years professionalism has been to seek the voices of students who have been at the heart of the various initiatives to improve the qualification base and range in the early years workforce. In general these studies demonstrate a widespread and deep commitment amongst students and professionals to the work that they do, confirming a sense of vocation and passion for working with young children and their families (Moyles, 2001; Hallett, 2013). Early years students and professionals are often defined quite significantly by an ethic of care (Osgood, 2006) at least as strong and perhaps more so than an educative orientation, leading Osgood to make the case for educators supporting students to become '*critically reflective emotional professionals*' (Osgood, 2010).

This deep and abiding commitment is well evidenced throughout the literature and is clearly something we need to bear in mind as educators in the early years but as Georgeson and Campbell-Barr (2015) remind us it is not something we can automatically take for granted amongst our students: '*there is a risk of assuming that if people have found their way on to an early childhood course, they very likely already have certain general dispositions*' (Georgeson and Campbell-Barr, 2015, p 323). Similarly, they will not necessarily hold commensurate views and values to our own and Georgeson and Campbell-Barr further caution educators to '*be wary of constructing what we view as the "good early years student"*' (ibid, p 329). If we are to hold to an ethic of sensitive and respectful ways to work with young children we will need to find it in ourselves to accord similar sensitivity and respect to the students we work with, whilst simultaneously opening up a professional dialogue around core professional principles and values.

As educators we may also find ourselves working with students who have been encouraged to sign up for courses by their managers and setting leaders but are not necessarily deeply committed to participating (Ingleby, 2018) or who are used to a more constrained and functional level of training and who believe that '*a lot of it is common sense*' (Vincent and Braun, 2011).

Reflection

Consider the following quotations from early years students included in Vincent and Braun's article (ibid, pp 778–779):

'*I don't think there's a course in this whole world, childcare course, that could teach you more than what you could learn once you're doing it.*'

'*Some of the theorists are so long ago that I think I probably find it difficult to think, "And we still agree with that?"*'

'*I do think a lot of it is common sense. I kept thinking, why do I have to write this down when it is common sense to do it…?*'

» How would you respond to such views and sentiments if you heard them amongst your students?

» Do you agree in part or do you disagree profoundly? Why do you feel that way and how should your views inform how you would respond to the students?

» How might you open up a wider debate about the need for less constrained visions of working in the early years?

One area of working with students that may be particularly helpful in rethinking these divides between theory and practice may be in the context of supervision of practice, although this may also be an arena where the functionalist and required elements of training, for instance in relation to safeguarding, can still dominate (Soni, 2018). It is of course perfectly valid and essential to give such aspects a high priority but Soni also argues powerfully for an integrated perspective that educators can take to supervision of placement in which they can emphasise the educative angle, taking the opportunity to breathe life into theory and to use practice to interrogate theory. They can also focus on experiences in practice to support students in the emotional demands of their role, a topic which we will return to later.

It is likely however that most of the students we work with as educators will be deeply imbued with the ethic of care and sustained by a genuine passion to enhance their own understanding and professional standing so as to further enhance their work with children and families. In this they may confront a paradox (Moyles, 2001) whereby their very commitment may bring them into conflict with some of the rather more instrumental aims and functions of early years education that the external political and business environment privileges and which are signposted in the next section.

Quality and competences

The drive towards greater levels of qualification amongst the early years workforce has been linked to a vein of research that demonstrates the significance of the early and pre-school years for improving the educational achievement of children and in particular the importance of early educational support to diminish the persistent levels of educational under-achievement of disadvantaged children that are evident in many countries. One of the most influential of these studies in the UK and beyond is the ground-breaking Effective Provision of Pre-school/Primary and Secondary Education (EPPSE) project that began in 1997 (Sylva et al, 2010). With an initial focus on the effective provision of pre-school education this major study tracked the impact of various types of pre-school provision for over 3000 children. It has been extended under successive governments enabling the research team to track the extended impact on children through primary and then into and through secondary school. One of the major factors to emerge from the study is the positive impact of graduate-level qualifications of early years staff on early and subsequent educational outcomes for children.

However this emphasis on *quality* of provision and the attendant link to measures of child performance is not uncontentious within the sector. Many dispute the ways in which policy-makers have interpreted and implemented policy based on this kind of research. One of the leading critics is Peter Moss, who has written extensively of the concern that an unremitting focus on early and narrowly defined educational outcomes detracts from a more holistic and balanced experience for young children that respects the integrity and meaning of this stage of life in itself and not simply as a preparation for other stages in life. Writing in 2016, Moss poses the question *'why can't we get beyond quality?'* (Moss, 2016) and reiterates a position shared by many amongst those researching early years that quality is a narrowly interpreted political choice and not a necessity. These authors argue that the fixation with a small number of cognitive and school-like measurable outcomes is driven by a politically oriented neo-liberal stance. It results in professional development and training being construed and configured in a *'technicist'* and instrumental fashion that privileges the pursuit of a set of narrow competencies rather than a holistic and more ethical approach to working with young children. One especially tense flashpoint for the clash of educational philosophies centres on the trend towards a school readiness focus at younger age ranges and *'schoolification'* of the early years, supported by training of professionals that emphasises these aims (Ang, 2014; Neaum, 2016).

Urban et al (2012), in reviewing early childhood provision and training in a pan-European project, addressed the question of what should be the core competencies of a professional working in the sector and concluded that there should indeed be a focus on child outcomes but these should relate also to families and the communities that settings serve and cannot be *'predetermined without negotiations with all stakeholders'* (p 510). This is a tall order and is not one that is easily laid at the feet of our students who may be juggling already very complex work–life–study commitments but as educators we need to determine how we at least make our students aware of such intense political and philosophical debates.

Reflection

» What do you think constitutes quality in the early years?

» How should early years settings best prepare children for school? Or do you believe that to do so undermines the very nature of the early years?

» How would you challenge students to think about what they are asked to do in settings that focus on the assessment of child outcomes and reporting of these?

» Is it your place to hone the ideological and philosophical standpoints of your students? Can you ethically not do so if the values you hold are at extreme variance to what you see your students being asked to do in practice?

These may not be easy dilemmas for either students or ourselves as educators to address and as Barron (2016) notes can produce *'stormy professional trajectories'*. Barron bases his conclusions on interviews with students training as EYTs, which highlighted the tension that can be experienced when they meet *'instrumental policy in practice'* (p 325) and struggle to reconcile their ideas and beliefs about ethical practices and their theoretical perspectives with tasks and practices they are being asked to fulfil in settings or that policy demands of them in settings. Barron calls for *'dialogism'* between students, Higher Education (HE) tutors and placement coordinators to surface rather than subsume these tensions. It is important to recognise that this type of dialogue can be a difficult line to hold since, as Barron notes, as educators we must also be aware that there are ethical dimensions in how we steer our students. After all, their career pathways will depend on them taking their place in a sector where their future success and that of the settings in which they will work will be judged by the prevalent discourses and the measurable outcomes that they underpin (Barron, ibid, p 337). As educators too, we may also find that many of the programmes on which we teach are driven by competence and skill-based policy imperatives and in that sense it is a dilemma that we may well share with our students. By entering into a dialogue and opening up the tensions for debate we may not find easy solutions to these dilemmas but we may bolster our students and our own ability to identify our core principles and to hold fast to those whilst discerning those areas where creative compromises might be made.

Emotional labour

One further theme that resonates through research into the professional identity and development of those working in the early years, which we touched on earlier, is the theme of emotional labour. Taggart (2015) revisits the term '*emotional labour*', used by Hochschild in the 1980s and which characterises the work of many in the caring professions. It is described by Taggart as the '*deliberate management of moral emotions such as compassion and patience for professional ends*' (Taggart, ibid, p 382). He explores the relevance of this term for those working in the early years sector, drawing attention to the strain that can be put upon professionals when they find their ability to act in compassionate and emotionally responsive ways is compromised by other demands of their job. Such strains can include the tensions derived from the type of external outcome-driven constraints and expectations, as described earlier, and which may conflict with their nurturing ethic and their instinct to want to act in a spirit of '*professional love*'.

He highlights the pressure too that may be placed upon educators who will need to find sensitive ways to address the relational aspects and dynamics of their students' daily work, helping them to practise a relational pedagogy and helping students to be attuned to the needs of children and to act appropriately and responsively. Taggart also argues that this emotional labour may cause stress and burnout in students and professionals as they may find it difficult to de-limit their own emotional involvement and to set realistic expectations of their own capacity to love and to give of themselves. One solution he offers is that pre-service training and indeed ongoing support for professionals might embrace some of the principles of mindfulness.

The emotional aspects of working in early years settings is a theme that has been well developed in the work of Peter Elfer, who has highlighted the depth of emotional response that can be evoked and felt by those working in often intense and relationally intimate ways with young children and their families (Elfer and Dearnley, 2007; Elfer, 2012a, 2015). Throughout this work Elfer and colleagues draw attention to the range of emotions that can be felt by professionals in such contexts that can be intensely negative as well as intensely positive. Sometimes these feelings will be experienced consciously but they may also be subconsciously present.

Reflection

» How might you advise a student who feels they are becoming too closely involved with the children or families with whom they work?

» How would you support and advise a student who feels guilty because they don't particularly like certain children or their families?

» How would you support a student in managing healthy working relationships with other adults in their settings?

» Similarly, how will you monitor and handle the emotions that the students with whom you work might arouse in you?

One approach that Elfer suggests is to develop an emotionally containing model of professional development that gives permission and time to consider such sensitive issues in an open and non-judgemental fashion. In his later works Elfer has also outlined a '*work discussion*' approach that ensures that both training and ongoing working contexts devote specific time for students and professionals to discuss and explore their emotional responses within the workplace. Such models do rely on a high degree of openness and trust which can take time to build. Depending on the mode of training this may not be easy to facilitate but as educators we can at least have an awareness of the potential and potent emotional labour that students may experience and be ready to respond empathetically.

Complex models

This chapter has introduced a number of dilemmas and issues that can challenge educators of early years students, which suggest that our approaches in working with students will need to be multi-faceted. Given the complexity of the roles our students face in their workplaces we cannot simply focus on competencies, final outcomes and credentials achieved. We will need to aspire towards more sustained and transformative forms of training (Osgood, 2006).

Brock (2012) offers a seven-fold typology of professionalism, which includes the acquisition of (i) knowledge, (ii) skills, (iii) qualifications and (iv) rewards, but also highlights the need to develop (v) values, (vi) ethics and (vii) autonomy. Similarly Molla and Nolan (2018) in their more recent study re-frame professional learning as requiring an expansive approach to develop capability across five domains, as noted below.

Reflection

Consider the five domains of professional development identified by Molla and Nolan:

i. *Expertise: specific knowledge and skills required in the profession;*

ii. *Deliberation: the ability to critically reflect on professional practice;*

iii. *Recognition: becoming valued for your role;*

iv. *Responsiveness: being able to meet diverse needs of children, drawing upon a disposition of social justice and being an agent for change;*

v. *Integrity: being respectful and respected in your professional practice and acting ethically.*

(Adapted from Molla and Nolan, 2018)

» In what ways does your practice as an educator in the early years facilitate and enable students to develop across all these dimensions?

» In what ways might you adapt your approaches and methods to bring this about?

» Are there other facets of being a professional that you feel are relevant to develop?

IN A **NUTSHELL**

There are challenges for educators in the early years driven by increasing imperatives to enhance '*quality*' in the early years through increasing the level of qualification in the EY workforce. This is a workforce which, more so than other phases of education, remains a very diverse and predominantly low-status profession. Additionally, there are very acute tensions about the ultimate aims of early years education and the appropriateness of the balance between education and care. Some of these tensions are exacerbated by and simultaneously exacerbate the emotional labour that characterises the early years workplace. For these reasons professional development is inevitably a complex phenomenon, which demands deep critical reflection and is likely to be best supported if undertaken in a spirit of positive professional dialogue.

REFLECTIONS ON **CRITICAL ISSUES**

The complexities outlined above require a book that is premised upon professional dialogue and this concept is expanded upon and explored in Chapter 2. This chapter also outlines the ways in which educators can encourage students to respond to contrasting visions and ideals of early years education. The chapter further highlights the significance of a reflective and engaged profession ready to enter into critical and informed dialogues with other professionals, policy-makers and those who access provision of all types.

Chapter 3 foregrounds the child as the most important starting position for early years care and education provision and considers how educators can support students to ensure that their decisions and practices have an ethical standpoint and are judiciously informed by some of the enduring traditions and philosophies in early years education. It gives suggestions as to how educators and students can explore these through research-informed critical debate.

Chapter 4 presents a relational model of learning that focuses on the interactions between children and adults and the structural features of their learning environments. The chapter presents a variety of research informed ideas about effective teaching and learning and developmentally informed practice in the early years and offers some parameters and guidance for how educators can help students to sift various forms of evidence and reach informed decisions.

Chapter 5 takes the focus outside of the immediate learning context and highlights how wider contextual influences and relationships impact on learning within settings. It showcases ways in which educators can work with students working in the early years to draw on these wider understandings and suggest ways in which students and professionals can engage in proactive dialogue with families and the communities in which their professional work is set.

Chapter 6 returns to the notion of what it means to be an informed professional in dialogue with others based on the diverse ideas encountered in Chapters 2–5. What does it mean to be an informed practitioner without being wedded to one set of ideas and practices? How can the practitioner make their own reasoned choices and simultaneously remain open to new ideas and innovative practices? This chapter includes suggestions for effective mentoring and coaching approaches that foster professional dialogue and development. It argues that such approaches can facilitate professional development for self and others and in so doing augment overall professional understanding and reflection and create new and positive ways of working across the sector workforce.

Further reading

BERA/TACTYC Early Childhood Research Review 2003–2017. [online] Available at: www.bera.ac.uk; www.tactyc.org.uk.

Elwick, A, Osgood, J, Robertson, L, Sakr, M and Wilson, D (2018) In Pursuit of Quality: Early Childhood Qualifications and Training Policy. *Journal of Education Policy,* 33(4): 510–525.

Harwood, D, Klopper, A, Osanyin, A and Vanderlee, M (2013) 'It's More Than Care': Early Childhood Educators' Concepts of Professionalism. *Early Years,* 33(10): 4–17.

Spencer, P, Harrop, S, Thomas, J and Cain, T (2018) The Professional Development Needs of Early Career Teachers, and the Extent to Which They Are Met: a Survey of Teachers in England. *Professional Development in Education,* 44(1): 33–46.

Waters, J and Payler, J (2015) The Professional Development of Early Years Educators: Achieving Systematic, Sustainable and Transformative Change. *Professional Development in Education,* 41(2): 161–168.

CHAPTER 2 | WHAT DOES PROFESSIONAL DIALOGUE MEAN?

Elise Alexander

CRITICAL ISSUES

- What is professional dialogue?
- Why is it important for early years educators?
- How can it be used in early years contexts?

Introduction

The quotation below is drawn from data collected in a research project that investigated early years practitioners' understandings of quality in their work with children. This head of a children's centre explains how she established a positive ethos in her setting based on principles and shared values through professional dialogue.

Res: Please tell me about the main aims or goals of this setting.

Head: We worked very strongly on our vision statement when I first came into post and I feel that we share a vision across the centre and it's really to…ensure high well-being and involvement, to promote fulfilment and play as key to children's learning, to celebrate flow and seamlessness and continuity and cohesion…to work alongside and with parents as partners, as far as possible…to talk and communicate and be open and available…(pause)…and to have high levels of learning.

Res: Can you talk me through the process, how you came together to arrive at this vision statement?

Head: Yeah, if I can remember (laughs) we had a whole day inset on the first day of term where I talked about why we were here, what we wanted, what our personal ethoses were for children and what we wanted our centre to be like. We worked in small groups and arrived at some purpose statements which we then refined and put into a page of what we wanted it to be like and then we refined that into a… I think it's probably a ten-point vision which we keep reviewing, we keep needing to remind ourselves of the vision.

Res = researcher; Head = head of children's centre

What is professional dialogue?

Professional dialogue, or professional conversation, is a means of building shared understanding and developing the capacity of teachers to build new knowledge, which in turns helps them to support change and improve their practice (Irvine and Price, 2014). These conversations become more significant and valuable when the existing knowledge and expertise of the participants is recognised and when there is belief in the collective intelligence or wisdom of the group. These elements contribute to the creation of a safe and supportive learning environment in which sufficient time and space are allowed for participants to critically reflect, to form and to share views. The process then allows the participants to move from surface to deeper knowledge and understanding (Brown and Isaacs, 2005; Stanfield, 2000; Tan and Brown, 2005).

Professional conversations take many forms, from the informal chat with a colleague that leads to a better understanding, or reflecting together, or a more formal process of structured dialogue in which coaching and mentoring is the aim. In my own work as an educator of early years students and professionals many conversations begin with questions or statements about learning and teaching. These conversations are not planned or organised, but nevertheless they are often valuable and informative, shaping my thinking and helping me to perceive issues in a new light.

Developing professional identity

Professional conversations and dialogue play an important role in the development of professional identity, which is a particularly complex process in the case of an early years teacher (Lightfoot and Frost, 2015). Discovering what kind of teacher you are and developing positive relationships with other teachers and educators, parents and, most importantly, children is complicated by the interplay between a number of elements. For teacher educators this is an important understanding that can be conveyed to students and requires reflective space and explicit opportunity for professional dialogues to be built into professional courses. It also requires some reflective space for ourselves as educators and mentors since our own professional identity is inextricably part of what we share and communicate to student-teachers and practitioners.

Professional identity in the early years, according to Dalli (2008), is composed of pedagogical beliefs, professional knowledge and collaborative relationships, in interaction with each other. Balancing what is learned in training, what is required by regulatory frameworks and what is required to fit into the setting in combination with personal values and beliefs leads to a dynamic and sometimes uncertain identification process. It seems clear, however, that professional conversations and reflection can play a powerful role in the development of a sound professional identity, as Bleach (2013) discovered in her account of a Continuing Professional Development (CPD) programme linked to the implementation of the Irish national quality and curriculum frameworks for early childhood education.

These frameworks are designed to be process-oriented rather than outcome-orientated, supporting educators in a quest for quality practice through reflection and shared learning.

In her account, Bleach (2013) reports on a development programme for early years educators in Ireland, which suggests that a combination of purposeful peer interaction and learning through action can lead to real improvements in the quality of provision in early years settings. The programme was based upon the identification of a particular issue in each of 14 community-based settings, which was addressed through an action plan. The action plan incorporated processes of continuous self-evaluation and professional dialogue, which appear to have profoundly changed the participants' sense of themselves as early years educators, bringing about a greater awareness of their professional knowledge and the value of sharing and learning together. Bleach's research points to the power of peer interactions in bringing about changes in self-perception and greater understanding of the participants' professional roles through professional dialogue and reflection.

Influences on professional identity

Reflection

Think about your professional identity and the values that underpin your work. These questions will help you to focus.

- » Which three principles do you feel are most important in working with children?
- » Why do these things matter to you?
- » Who or what is the greatest influence on your sense of yourself as a teacher?
- » How do you enact these values in your work with students and professionals?

Share these thoughts with a colleague and perhaps your students too.

Professional dialogue is a powerful means of developing professional knowledge and identity, particularly when it is owned by educators as they develop shared understandings about what works in particular settings. It is also being recognised by some governments. These include the Irish frameworks, which formed the basis of Bleach's study and also an Australian initiative, the National Quality Framework outlined by Irvine and Price (2014).

Professional dialogue and quality in the early years

To understand how professional dialogue helps to improve quality it is important to first explore the nature of quality in the early years. Early years services, their planning, regulation and funding are subject to unprecedented scrutiny in the UK and quality is promoted through a range of targets and professional standards. It is perhaps comforting to see quality simply in terms of achieving *Outstanding* grades in Ofsted inspections and satisfying to meet regulatory standards. But are these supposedly objective measures of quality really providing a true picture of quality in early years settings?

It could be argued that the provision required to meet the standards of the range of regulatory frameworks that operate in the UK should, in all fairness, be regarded as the minimum entitlement for young children. After all, every setting has to achieve them so as to remain open. This proposition, however, carries the implication that a setting that achieves all the regulatory standards required of it might still only be providing the minimum quality provision to which children are entitled. Furthermore, Tanner and her colleagues (Tanner et al, 2006) point out that ideas about what constitutes quality are inextricably entwined with individual values and with the goals of childcare, which in turn are rooted in a range of understandings about the nature of childhood. It follows, then, that measures of quality are not genuinely objective and measurable, as the standards and regulatory frameworks propound, but instead they are subjective and open to interpretation. This can be a significant distinction to be explored with students and professionals and provides an excellent prompt for thinking about their underpinning values and emerging professional identities.

The findings from an Economic and Social Research Council (ESRC)-funded research project investigating early years practitioners' understandings of quality (RES-061-23-0012) support Tanner and her colleagues' hypothesis. In settings where practitioners saw themselves as engaged in the project of providing the best education and care for the children with whom they worked, staff described quality as a dynamic process which might never be completely achieved but nevertheless formed a crucial professional quest for the team. The practitioners in the best settings visited in the study (Cottle and Alexander, 2012) developed cultures in which debate and what MacNaughton terms '*positive dissensus*' (MacNaughton, 2005) emerged. Rather than aiming for consensus, MacNaughton argues, settings create a culture in which '*diversity flourishes, ruptures, reshoots and produces desires to transform the disrespectful, the inequitable and the joyless in children's lives*' (MacNaughton, 2005, p 153). In the settings we encountered in the Quality project (Cottle and Alexander, 2012) practitioners constructed, deconstructed and reconstructed their understandings as a team, constantly talking about the children, their observations and discussing next steps, so that everyone understood the values and priorities of the setting as a whole. In each of these settings, the ethos was one of healthy discussion and argument in the pursuit of better experiences and services for children and their families. But as well as healthy discussion and positive debate, practitioners embracing positive dissensus also have to embrace uncertainty and ambiguity and, perhaps, conflict. Uncertainty and ambiguity are much easier to manage and less threatening if shared with a team of like-minded practitioners.

In interviews, the leaders of these settings talked of the importance of positive relationships, which, to them, were essential if the culture of positive dissensus was to thrive. Positive dissensus, however, in no way lessens the importance of positive relationships in high-quality settings. Indeed, there was evidence in the focus groups and in the interview data from the participants that an ethos of constant quest for improvement was only possible in a climate that fostered positive relationships in the team, between parents and practitioners and also between practitioners and children.

When is professional dialogue useful?

Professional dialogue can be helpful in a number of contexts: when you are new in a setting, to find out how things are done there; as you settle in and find you need to think more deeply about the children and how you work with them and their families and with other staff. Later still, perhaps you assume leadership and have to manage change and development in the setting. At some point you may also have responsibility for training and mentoring those new to early years care and education work as well as established teachers and practitioners or leaders of settings who are moving on to the next stage in their own professional journey. In all these situations, professional dialogue is a valuable tool which helps you to understand your own thinking as well as the thoughts, ideas and concerns of the people with whom you work.

It can be disorientating to discover that knowledge gained in training and education at any stage of professional status may not be a perfect match for the ethos and practice of the settings and contexts in which you find yourself working. In this situation training and experience can create a sound basis from which to navigate professional norms and expectations in the classroom or setting, but developing an understanding of the shared values and priorities of the setting and, indeed, aligning these with your own values can perhaps best be achieved through a process of professional dialogue.

Conducting professional dialogue

Professional dialogue takes many forms, including informal, spontaneous conversations with colleagues and internal dialogue – talk for oneself – which is revealed more clearly through reflection. Then there is more formal reflection, which takes place in professional groups and in coaching activities. In all these forms, professional dialogue has most value when we recognise that it is happening and take note of what we discover in the process. For those training others the dialogue with students and professionals provides a further forum for such reflection and dialogue. Each new cohort of students and each individual student can reinforce or challenge our views and values and in so doing develop our own professional identity.

Conversations with colleagues

Conversations are often overlooked as a means of professional learning, probably because they form such a constant thread in our personal and professional lives. We spend so much time in conversation that it is easy to take conversational learning for granted. The ways in which conversation differs from other forms of professional conversation, according to Haigh (2005), include the serendipitous nature of the exchanges, the immediacy of the topic (these conversations are seldom planned in advance so they are often about topics that are of concern or interest to the participants) and often include storytelling and anecdotes. They are also generally experienced as non-threatening, and the openness of the exchange can encourage radical thinking and risk-taking, which may not be encouraged or fostered in a more formal discussion.

Conversations may not be highly valued in this age of evidence-based education precisely because of their informality and anecdotal nature, but they are nevertheless an integral part of professional life as they are essential to the formation of professional relationships and, arguably, to the development of an individual's professional identity.

Of course, conversation can easily shift and change into something else, a monologue for example, or an opportunity to lecture a colleague on one's favourite topic. There are a number of conversational protocols that many of us use unconsciously: showing friendly interest in colleagues' views, being aware that we are taking up their valuable time or leaving opportunities for them to respond. All these small considerations help conversations to develop and move smoothly as equal and mutually satisfying exchanges.

Senge draws our attention to the dangers of unfettered conversation, however, corralling the concept with the phrase '*learningful conversation*' and characterising the ability to engage in such conversation as a pre-requisite for learning (Senge, 1994). Conversations are more likely to support professional learning if they take the form of dialogue rather than discussion, in which one person is likely to become the leader in shaping the conversation. This, Senge claims, is because dialogue involves participants in exploration and consideration of the attitudes, assumptions and reasons for a particular point of view or opinion (Senge, 1994). Dialogue then becomes the starting point for a conversation in which it is easy to review your stance, modify assumptions and even change your mind completely in relative safety.

Conversations may also be the crucibles of creativity, opening possibilities of improvisation, new insights and vivid re-imagining. Conversations about ideas involve interactions with others, which have the potential to transform our thinking. Theodore Zeldin (1998) frames this notion rather poetically:

Conversation is a meeting of minds with different memories and habits. When minds meet, they don't just exchange facts; they transform them, draw different implications from them, and engage in new trains of thought. Conversation doesn't just reshuffle the cards; it creates new cards.

Reflective writing

Writing is not the only way of reflecting but it is powerful, can be done alone and has unique advantages. Not least, you can use reflective writing to make use of apparently casual conversations with colleagues, which often provide serendipitous opportunities for professional development.

Professional dialogue could also begin with an internal dialogue – a conversation with oneself, or perhaps a continuation of a conversation with a colleague recollected and reflected upon through writing. Keeping a reflective journal is a powerful means of recording your thoughts so that you can get them into the open and scrutinise them. Bassot ascribes the metaphor of a mirror to the reflective process, a mirror which heightens your levels of self-awareness and critical evaluation as you examine your knowledge, skills and attitudes (Bassot, 2013). Writing, Bassot claims, is much more than a conversation with oneself; it can lead to a significantly deeper level of reflection because it slows down thought processes and the transition from thought to written word actually demands deep reflection. Because reflective writing is such a powerful tool in professional dialogue, I have included some detailed notes about how to write reflectively and how to use your writing to develop your professional identity. Such techniques and guidance are valuable assets that can be passed on to students to promote and foster their own self-reflection and inner dialogue.

To start a reflective journal, Bolton (2010) suggests the following ideas to help students begin.

» *Write whatever is in your head.*
» *Time yourself and write for six minutes without stopping.*
» *Don't be critical of your writing, even if it does not appear to make sense.*
» *Let it flow.*
» *Give yourself permission to write about anything at all.*
» *Remember that what you write cannot be wrong – it belongs to you and no one else needs ever to read it.*

Once the student has written about what is concerning, intriguing or exciting her, the next stage is to analyse the account, which is the most complex and difficult part of the process. Bassot (2013) suggests the following questions as a guide.

» *What is happening here?*
» *What assumptions am I making?*
» *What does this suggest about my underlying beliefs about myself and my practice?*
» *Are there other ways of looking at this? Is there another perspective?*

When the student has reflected upon her analysis, which might mean more writing, she could use the reflections to decide upon action, to reflect further on what she has learned or to make plans to avoid similar situations arising in future. This type of writing can also form a useful starting point for discussion with and between students.

Example of reflective writing

The following extract is from a reflective essay written by a student who is new to a placement in an early years setting. She reflects on her experience of a Stay and Play session, in which children and parents interact, in the setting:

During Stay and Play the practitioner I was shadowing took a Consumer Model approach (in which parents are in control of the relationship between themselves and Early Years practitioners); as they were not leading any activities they mainly stayed in one place, at the end of the room, while the parents played with their children at the other. Communication happened when the parents approached the practitioners with specific questions.

Maybe some parents are not looking for close relationships with practitioners, but I feel a bit disorientated by these reflections. I wrote in my journal:

'I did not really know what I was meant to be doing. All the children were busy with their parents and all the parents were either with their children or in conversations with other parents'.

Reflection

These questions may help to guide students' reflections.

» Does the student's reflective essay and log resonate with your experience of working with parents?

» Why might parents choose not to engage with practitioners during Stay and Play?

» Should practitioners in this situation take action? If so, what action should they take? Why should they take this action?

» What do you think about the relationship between staff and parents in an early years setting? Why do you hold your particular set of beliefs?

John Dewey thought a great deal about reflection. These are his four main criteria for good reflection, distilled by Carol Rogers.

1. *Reflection is a meaning-making process that moves a learner from one experience into the next with deeper understanding of its relations with and connections to other experiences and ideas. It is the thread that makes continuity of learning*

possible and ensures the progress of the individual and, ultimately, society. It is a means to essentially moral ends.

2. *Reflection is a systematic, rigorous, disciplined way of thinking with its roots in scientific inquiry.*

3. *Reflection needs to happen in community, in interaction with others.*

4. *Reflection requires attitudes that value the personal and intellectual growth of oneself and others.*

(Rogers, 2002, p 845)

It is clear from these criteria that Dewey recognised the power of reflection, but also recognised the professional attitudes that are fundamental to successful, positive professional dialogue.

The risk in reflective writing

A valuable dimension of reflection is the moral element, mentioned above in Dewey's first criterion. Reflection can help you to identify your biases, preconceptions and assumptions, and it can also help you to resolve ethical issues and, ultimately, can lead to forgiveness, both of yourself and of others. For example, reflection can help to explore the practice of colleagues that you find difficult to understand: why do they act in ways that do not accord with your values or the ethos of the setting? Perhaps they are working from a different philosophical basis. Perhaps you have identified a feature of practice that you wish to change. Perhaps you might have been wrong about this particular aspect of practice all along. Perhaps you find yourself questioning your beliefs, your practice and, indeed, your professional identity, which may be an uncomfortable or even painful process.

There is an element of risk involved in reflective writing. Even if no one else reads what you write, there are still risks attached to writing honestly and reflectively. It might be worth getting your students to consider the risks inherent in reflective writing by addressing the following questions.

» How might you mitigate these risks?
» How might you use them to enhance your professional learning?
» How might these risks help you to reframe your professional identity?

So how do we manage the moral and ethical dimensions of reflection in reflective writing? Swarbrick and Mitchell write in detail about ethics in relation to professional dialogue in Chapter 3. It is important, however, to emphasise the importance of principles when conducting professional conversations: elements of trust, respect and generosity are integral to the process of professional development through dialogue. Bolton reminds us that positive regard, the sense we retain of others as professional colleagues engaged in the same project of care and education as we are, is vital to the development of positive professional identity (Bolton, 2010). We are, after all, discussing lots of different people when we engage in professional dialogue – colleagues, children, parents of children.

In our efforts to understand what has happened and if we are to maintain positive professional relationships in future, it is important to also maintain respect for all those involved.

As teacher educators too we must be mindful of the views and sensitivities of the students and professionals whom we work with and of the multiplicity of views that we may encounter in our own professional teaching. How do we foster dialogue and debate that enables a variety of views to be expressed and discussed? At what point might we decide that the professional dialogue unfolding before us needs to be extended or conversely to be countered and possibly curtailed? What are the underlying power dynamics within our own teaching contexts and how do we accord genuine respect for different views and foster a spirit of free debate whilst simultaneously being an advocate for what we believe to be best practice?

Reflection in/on practice, together

The head of a children's centre, whose words opened this chapter, describes how she created an opportunity for the staff in her setting to reflect on their professional values and use the shared understanding they developed to create a cohesive set of values or principles. It is important to note that these values are not seen as fixed and static, nor do they form a '*mission statement*'; instead they are reviewed and revised regularly in a continuous process of professional dialogue.

Reflecting together is immensely useful for questioning practice, developing professional identity and also articulating values. It may not be possible to ensure that everyone subscribes to all the values and principles created by the staff team, but the process of articulation ensures that everyone's perspective is aired and discussed. Bleach comments that the empowerment experienced by practitioners in the process of group reflection was one of the most valued outcomes of her continuous professional development (CPD) programme precisely because everyone involved felt their thoughts and feelings were given weight and significance (Bleach, 2013).

Professional dialogue in groups is clearly valuable for addressing complex questions of principle or practice, but to be effective it is important to pay attention to the nature of the questions posed for consideration. If the questions under consideration can be answered with a simple '*yes*' or '*no*', they are probably not nuanced enough to provoke deep thinking in the participants. Open questions following a semi-structured format allow participants to interpret and explore the topic, challenging their thinking and encouraging them to take ownership of the views expressed and, indirectly, of any changes in practice that result. This open-ended format also allows the lead participants to be open to the ideas expressed by the others, creating a genuinely reciprocal dialogue.

Reflection

Consider these questions about working with parents in early years settings.

» Is working with parents simply a matter of good communication?

» Do you think that early childhood education and care staff think that caring for and educating children is their primary task, and communicating with parents is a secondary role? (MacNaughton and Hughes, 2011)

» Which of these questions would be more appropriate for discussion in professional dialogue? Why? How did you decide?

Reflecting in groups inevitably involves the giving and receiving of feedback from colleagues. Ideally, each member of the team involved in professional dialogue could speak honestly and constructively about weaknesses, problems and other emotionally charged issues and their words would be received equally constructively and with an open mind. This discursive plateau may take some time to achieve however; as a culture of professional dialogue is being established, ground rules may be necessary to foster a culture of constructive professional dialogue. These ground rules should be negotiated as part of the professional dialogue process so that all participants own them.

IN A **NUTSHELL**

Professional dialogue is a powerful way to support professional development. This is particularly important for early years educators and teacher educators whose professional identity may comprise complex dynamic factors. Effective professional dialogue may include reflective writing as well as professional conversations, with respect, honesty and constructive acceptance at the heart of all forms.

REFLECTIONS ON **CRITICAL ISSUES**

This chapter has explored the power of professional dialogue as a tool to support the development of professional identity in early years educators. Professional identity in the early years is a complex interaction between an educator's pedagogical beliefs, professional knowledge and collaborative relationships in the workplace (Dalli, 2008). As such, professional conversations between educators in an early years context assume great significance, not only for individual educators but also for building a collective positive ethos.

Further reading

Chalke, J (2013) Will the Early Years Professional Please Stand Up? Professionalism in the Early Childhood Workforce in England. *Contemporary Issues in Early Childhood,* 14(3): 212–222.

Murray, J (2013) Becoming an Early Years Professional: Developing a New Professional Identity. *European Early Childhood Education Research Journal,* 21(4): 527–540.

Trodd, L and Dickerson, C (2018) 'I Enjoy Learning': Developing Early Years Practitioners' Identities as Professionals and as Professional Learners. *Professional Development in Education.* DOI: 10.1080/19415257.2018.1459788.

CHAPTER 3 | REVISITING VALUES AND ETHICAL STANDPOINTS IN EARLY YEARS EDUCATION

Helena Mitchell and Nick Swarbrick

CRITICAL ISSUES

- What are your underlying ethical beliefs about practice in the early years?
- Why are ethical beliefs important, and how do they impact on your work with young children?
- How do ethical beliefs impact on your work in the early years?

Introduction

In Chapter 2, Alexander explored the notions of professional identity and the place of professional dialogue in developing that identity. In this chapter we want the reader to explore their own ethical stance about education: it is important that the decisions you make when working with students (or with children and their parents, or with the rest of the school community) are underpinned by your own beliefs and values, which are a critical element of developing professional identity. These, therefore, are the issues we want to discuss.

The importance of the culture and context for early learning should not be underestimated. The early years of life are crucial in establishing the ways in which children learn and develop, and the child's experience must be central to the philosophy and practice of their education. Fisher (2013, p 10) states:

Young children come to make sense of their world by observing, imitating, investigating and exploring. They learn attitudes, skills, strategies and concepts that enable them to be understood.

Fisher's work draws upon many of the tenets of early education, including Maslow's hierarchy of needs, initially introduced in 1943, which highlights the importance of meeting basic needs such as food and shelter as well as safety and positive relationships as precursors for effective learning. Fisher's view of the child is as an active interrogator of the environment, seeking to learn through discovery and interaction with others, both adults and children.

As an educator, your view of the child and the child's potential for learning is crucial in your view of how that learning can be achieved. Your views are underpinned by your beliefs, and in order to understand those you need to explore their origin and impact upon your work, and the wider professional context in which you are working. The term '*attitudes*' is often used to describe the way that educators perceive their role, and the ways in which they may view the children with whom they are working. The term '*dispositions*' is also found in literature about early childhood and is often used interchangeably with '*attitudes*'. Katz (1993, cited by Georgeson and Campbell-Barr, 2015, p 16), provides the following definitions: '*Attitudes are relatively enduring organizations of beliefs*' and dispositions are '*a pattern of behaviour*'. These definitions provide a clear separation of the two terms, but highlight the way in which individual understanding and use of terminology may vary. So, we are examining terms such as beliefs, values, philosophies, attitudes, ethics and dispositions. The ways in which these are sometimes used interchangeably is often confusing. The word '*dispositions*' is usually used when describing children's behaviour, whereas the terms '*beliefs*', '*values*', '*philosophies*' and '*ethics*' are likely to apply to the educator's stance. In this chapter we are focusing on ethics, whilst acknowledging that interchangeability is a feature of the literature, and indeed, of common usage. So, what do we mean by beliefs?

Reflection

Examine the terminology and consider what it means to you.

» You might start by writing down an example for yourself of something which is a belief for you. For example, do you believe that young children are competent learners? Why do you have this belief? Share your chosen belief with a colleague or friend.

» Why did you choose this example? Why is it important to you? Why is it one of your beliefs?

» How far does your belief coincide with that of your colleague or friend? Is it a source of agreement or disagreement?

As an educator you may find that your students have different underlying beliefs. As a mentor, you need to ensure that you have a strategy for exploring these differences, and supporting your students to examine and appraise them critically.

Some definitions

What do the following terms mean to you?

» *Ethics*

» *Values*

» *Beliefs*

Are they clearly defined or do they overlap? Is it difficult to distinguish one from another? The use of a reflective journal, as explained in Chapter 2, can be very helpful here.

Values are based on beliefs and link to ethical standpoints. *The Cambridge English Dictionary* defines values as '*the principles that help you to decide what is right and wrong, and how to act in various situations*'.

Cribb (2009) believes that each profession has a set of '*values and virtues*' designed to serve particular ends, which can be described as professional ethics. Such professional ethics (or values) often have underlying principles. Campbell (2003, p 12) lists the following: '*Fairness, integrity, moral courage, compassion, honesty, patience*'. Furthermore '*Beliefs can act as filters because they are considered to influence all other knowledge and beliefs*' (Lunn Brownlee et al, 2016, p 263). So beliefs are personal, and exist alongside each other, even though one may contradict and challenge another.

Ethics, according to moral and ethical theory, is what makes an action right but this is a simplistic definition. Moreover, there is a difference between personal and professional ethics, in that professional requirements may stipulate a certain course of action that may challenge a personal ethical standpoint. So, for example, the professional requirement to administer a test to all children may challenge a personal belief that testing for young children is inappropriate. Thus challenges about ethics, values and beliefs are constantly likely to be in play in professional situations, and will underpin decision making. Taggart (2011) discusses the complexity of the '*ethics of care*', and the challenges it provides.

Leadership positions too require the acknowledgement of the underlying ethical stance, which is governing practice and the need for exploration of the team's agreement on these if practice is to be consistent and equitable.

Beliefs about teaching and learning are often multi-dimensional and different beliefs may co-exist, together forming a personal epistemology. Dewey, in 1897 (http://dewey.pragmatism.org/creed.htm), sets out a string of beliefs about education and schooling such as

I believe that this educational process has two sides – one psychological and one sociological…I believe that the psychological and social sides are organically related and that education cannot be regarded as a compromise between the two, or a superimposition of one upon the other…

I believe that much of present education fails because it neglects this fundamental principle of the school as a form of community life. It conceives the school as a place where certain information is to be given, where certain lessons are to be learned, or where certain habits are to be formed…

I believe that every teacher should realize the dignity of his calling.

Some of the values and beliefs we work with are consciously handed to us. They may be negotiated in how they are lived out, but they might come from government or local leadership. The Early Years Foundation Stage (EYFS) sprang from a desire in the 1990s to give clarity to the status of the learning of Nursery and Reception age children: Ofsted's early guidance technical paper (Tech paper 11) became first the Desirable Learning Outcomes (DLOs), 1996, in which end points for early learning were defined for England (and Wales); these were replaced in England, after some negotiation, by the Curriculum Guidance (QCA 2000) and in Wales in 2008.

The revision that followed in England produced a series of interesting documents (DfES, 2007) but this was felt by many to be too complex and unwieldy, and was revised following Dame Clare Tickell's view of the Early Years Foundation Stage (EYFS) in 2011 (Tickell, 2011).The latest government-determined Early Years Foundation curriculum documentation (DfE, 2017) was revised over four years (www.bera.ac.uk/wp-content/uploads/2017/05/BERA-TACTYC-Full-Report.pdf).

The latest documentation begins with the aspirational statement:

Every child deserves the best possible start in life and the support that enables them to fulfil their potential. Children develop quickly in the early years and a child's experiences between birth and age five have a major impact on their future life chances. A secure, safe and happy childhood is important in its own right. Good parenting and high quality early learning together provide the foundation children need to make the most of their abilities and talents as they grow up.

The British Association of Early Childhood Education has a similar statement on its website:

Early Education believes every child deserves the best possible start in life and support to fulfil their potential. A child's experience in the early years has a major impact on their future life chances. A secure, safe and happy childhood is important in its own right, and provides the foundation for children to make the most of their own abilities and talents as they grow up.

(www.early-education.org.uk/ethics-principles)

Embedded within these statements are implications about the way in which young children experience their childhood, and the ways in which the adults they encounter, including carers and educators, provide appropriate contexts and experiences. This crucial importance of understanding family and cultural contexts for early learning is explored further by Gilson in Chapter 5. From the perspective of the educator, the ways in which you engage with young children and what you will encourage your students to do relates to the educators' personal beliefs and philosophy about children's development and early learning. Alexander has already explored the notion of professional identity in Chapter 2 and its meaning and significance for educators. Additionally, the beliefs and philosophy that underpin that professional identity is often tacit, and educators may not be fully aware of the reasons for their beliefs and actions.

The Early Years Foundation Stage also re-states the importance of relationships, and of environment:

» [C]hildren learn to be strong and independent through positive relationships;

» [C]hildren learn and develop well in enabling environments, in which their experiences respond to their individual needs and there is a strong partnership between practitioners and parents and/or carers.

(EYFS, March 2017)

Reflection

In working with students it can be useful to draw attention to underlying beliefs behind examples of practice and policies they encounter. The following questions may be useful prompts to discuss with students.

» How does your nursery or school welcome babies or young children who are starting in the setting or school?

» What is the policy underpinning practice? Are there home visits made in advance? How do you liaise with parents and carers?

» Is the environment in your nursery or school an enabling environment?

» How does the partnership between educators and parents or carers operate in that environment?

» As the educator what sorts of responses will you be hoping for from the students? How will you help them to interrogate the underlying ethics and beliefs in these examples?

Fundamental British values

A further dimension of the debate around ethics, values and beliefs is the UK government's Prevent strategy, introduced in 2014, which incorporates the notion of fundamental British values (FBV), which all educators, and students, have been required to promote since that date. FBV are defined as: '*democracy, the rule of law, individual liberty, and mutual respect and tolerance of those with different faiths and beliefs*' (DfES, 2013, cited by Sant and Hanley, 2018).

In this context the interpretation of British values gains significance, and emphasises the need to understand and interpret one's own values. Sant and Hanley (2018), in a very small-scale study of secondary English student teachers, demonstrate the challenge for their student-teacher participants in defining what Britishness means to them. The variety of responses indicates the personal and cultural nature of interpretation, and the ways in which these affect their practice.

If we assume that student teachers are likely to support civic values such as democracy, tolerance etc., then spaces for pedagogical discussion need to be created so they can explore how certain pedagogies can or cannot contribute to these principles.

(Sant and Hanley, 2018, p 334)

Similarly, for educators and student teachers working with early years children, the government requirements in FBV require an understanding of and engagement with the policy. In her study, Robson (2017) examined the ways in which those educators working with young children interpreted the policy requirements and provided practical everyday examples of practice. The evidence from these studies is supported by Janmaat (2018) whose interrogation of data from the Citizenship Education Longitudinal Study (CELS) also showed a high proportion of 23 year-olds in the sample were very supportive of the four FBV values.

Balancing ethics, values and beliefs with policy

So the importance of knowing and understanding your own values and beliefs cannot be underestimated. Rayner (2014), in a small-scale study of headteachers, states that school leaders are influenced by their personal history in the ways in which they build their policy and practice. The difficulties of balancing their ethical perspective with some elements of policy were challenging at times. The need for clear underlying beliefs and a willingness to advocate for them was crucial. In Chapter 2, Alexander presents a vignette from her own research of the importance of the headteacher's vision for her children's centre in order to deliver high-quality education in the setting. This too was achieved by working collaboratively with colleagues. Consider the following issue, and examine your values and beliefs in this hypothetical context.

Reflection

A dilemma to share with your students: *'Bring back the infants'*.

The Leadership Team is looking to reshape the experience of the children in the first years of school. The headteacher explains to the staff she wants to 'bring back the infants'. There is a lot of talk in staff meetings and informally about what this appeal to nostalgia could look like in practical terms.

» Do you agree with it?

» What could it look like for you?

- » Do you envisage this in terms of provision and activity (for instance, more access to exploratory play activities inside and out) or in terms of approach (maybe through enhancing opportunities for children to initiate talk)?
- » What are the markers for you of a high-quality early years provision?
- » As the educator how will you respond if one or more of your students hold a different view to your own?

Early years philosophies

Early years practice does not arise from the ether, and is not a fixed set of practices. Despite this fluidity, it works. Historical perspectives, for example, help us query our current practices and beliefs. When we read about Margaret McMillan's impassioned vision of education we have to ask if her views of a provision that encourages health and imagination is at the heart of our own practice. Her open air nursery

rings with laughter and tripping of little feet... On the tables and along the walls there is apparatus of varied kinds, coloured discs, coloured balls, insets, colour scales, bright letters to be fitted, pictures and picture-books. Outside there are sliding boards, steps and rib stalls. All the best apparatus is in the garden...The two-year-old works hard. He and she have so much to learn. It is hard to stop him.

(McMillan, 1919, pp 4–5)

There are strong and resounding values and beliefs underlying practice in the early years that have been developed through the work of practitioners and psychologists, and in some cases, developed into government policies and practice. In translating the sources for our practice we have, of course, to filter the language: our own curriculum descriptions do not refer, as McMillan does, to how '*the Sun God...brings His great healing and joy to our children*' (ibid, p 5). Nevertheless, we might still believe that sunshine and fresh air are the '*birthright*' of the children in our charge, and if this is the case, why do we think this is so? Are we following in the line of '*nursery inheritance*' (Brooker, 2005, p 117, in Yelland, 2005) or using phrases and ideas from other times and other places to justify our own pedagogy? How do we justify and enact our own beliefs and values?

While not wanting necessarily to suggest a course in the history of early years ideology, it is worth noting how writers such as Tina Bruce have explored these roots, and you may want to ensure your students reflect on the influence of Friedrich Froebel, Susan Isaacs and Maria Montessori: the notions of developmentally appropriate practice and the place of play; the importance of the child's emotional life; the social roots of the Early Childhood Education project – these all sit behind the decisions we make on a daily basis when working with children and families. The importance of play-based learning is emphasised, and the need for the educator to scaffold children's learning, by assessing current knowledge and extending and developing it. However, Kwon (2002) discusses the notion of Western child-centred education and cites challenges to the theories, stating that free play has limitations and that research evidence has shown children do not necessarily persist at self-chosen tasks. Different perspectives are a fundamental part of life. The prescribed curriculum, the school structure and context, and the vision and beliefs of the leadership team are critical elements in the approaches taken within a school or setting. You will need to help your students to appreciate the need to explore the evidence and evaluate it in order to decide on their own values, beliefs and practice, and in order to advocate for the best way forward for the children in their care:

If you are working in a school like me, you cannot just sit back and do what you are told. At the end of the day for the children, this is a crucial year in their life. I am responsible for their progress. I have got to stick up for them, no matter what the others say or think of me.

(Beth; aged 26–30; PGCE Student, quoted in Silberfeld and Mitchell, 2018, p 12).

This becomes particularly important when our students are faced with initiatives they may feel uncomfortable enacting. How do you give them the confidence to stand by their beliefs to support or oppose this or that project for the benefit of the children they have responsibility for? Conversely, what if they simply assume they can incorporate curricular ideas that they would like to advocate for example such as Forest School from Scandinavia or child-centred creativity akin to that which those in the role of the *atelierista* in the Reggio Emilia approach to early years encourage? Making choices and facing dilemmas throughout the day represent a spectrum of choices that our students will be called upon to make and as educators we seek to give them an ethical foundation from which to do so.

Putting beliefs into practice

Building positive relationships and enabling environments requires educators to commit to a sound and strong philosophy, which underpins their work and to be active in finding ways to incorporate an ethical awareness into the experiences they open up to children.

For example, much of children's literature exploring beliefs and ethics in early education is concerned with providing examples for working with children that illustrate issues or everyday events. One children's book, *Titch*, by Pat Hutchins, has three children working together to plant a seed (held by Titch), which grows into a magnificent plant. The simple storyline is delightful, enabling Titch, the youngest of the three children, to play a major role, and emphasises everyone's contribution, and the relationship between the three. A story such as *Titch* emphasises positive relationships and so helps to build positive attitudes in an enabling environment. As an educator you may find yourself constantly on the lookout for such materials to share with your students and finding ways to encourage group pooling of ideas, such as children's book-sharing circles, can be very helpful and a very enjoyable part of an educator's role too. Of course the circle may not always concur about the ethical stances or values portrayed in such literature but this can be a useful way to open up dialogue about differing ideas because the focus is on a text rather than overt personal beliefs and it can be a very facilitative forum for discussion.

On a broader level, the amalgamation of the Birth to Three curriculum with the Early Learning Goals (for three- to five-year-olds) in 2006 brought into being the first curriculum for all young children across the age range in England. The new curriculum brought together elements of excellent practice based on the underlying beliefs that young children were active learners. According to Sylva et al (2004), a balance between teacher-initiated activity and potentially instructive play-based activities was demonstrated by the most successful educators, Additionally, it highlighted the importance of effective child–teacher interaction in early learning, whereby the educator scaffolds the child's learning, assessing the child's knowledge and extending and developing it through guidance and questioning. These themes are picked up in Chapter 4 but it is worth noting how curricula are informed by underlying beliefs in the way in which children learn and the ethics of '*interacting or interfering*' (Fisher, 2016). Approaches can differ too for historical and cultural reasons; for instance Scandinavian models tend to foreground child-centred early education, with a strong practical curriculum, but are less child-centred than the Reggio Emilia *atelierista* mode. Curricula and practice in different countries reflect the culture and values of that country, or, in the case of Reggio Emilia, a small city in northern Italy.

The Reggio Emilia Approach is an educational philosophy based on the image of the child, and of human beings, as possessing strong potentials for development and as a subject of rights who learns and grows in the relationships with others.

(www.reggiochildren.it/identita/reggio-emilia-approach/?lang=en)

The New Zealand Early years' curriculum Te Whariki perhaps tells us a great deal about cultural perspectives on learning, with an interwoven curriculum designed to bring together the varied culture and history of the country. Trying to import practice from another country or region, as some have tried to do with Reggio Emilia, is a huge challenge because that practice is embedded in the culture, ethics, values and beliefs of that country. However, as an educator finding ways to introduce the perspectives and traditional practices from elsewhere in the world or indeed in communities more locally can be another powerful way to support discussion and dialogue amongst students about their own beliefs and values. Sometimes these may be implicit based on their own upbringing and experiences rather than an explicit adherence to a particular model. Equally, being receptive to the differing perspectives that students may themselves bring can be an exciting element of being an educator.

Reflection

» Do you think there are any dominant cultural perspectives regarding early years care and education in the UK? If so, can you identify these?

» What evidence do you have for your beliefs? Do they underpin or challenge your practice?

» How would you introduce students to differing perspectives and how will you use this to challenge or strengthen their own deep seated views?

Compassionate leadership

In recent years, there has been an increasing emphasis on the importance of leadership in early years. During the early part of this century, with the expansion of Children's Centres, a new professional qualification, the National Professional Qualification in Integrated Centre Leadership (NPQICL), was introduced, along with Early Years Professional Status (EYPS), the latter for those educators who were leading practice in their schools and settings. EYPS has now been replaced by the Early Years Teacher, a level six qualification, which is aimed at those students working with Foundation Stage and Reception Year children. Both of these were designed for early education environments, and sought to develop a new, more compassionate and more distributed leadership model. Murray and McDowall Clark (2013, p 292) discuss the nature of this model, and the need for

[a]n open concept of leadership which encourages participation and empowers all, regardless of position.

Having a leadership role when working with young children has been highlighted by Elfer (2013) as requiring a high level of personal commitment and requiring a compassionate approach to staff and children. The notion of compassionate approaches has gained increasing importance. As noted in Chapter 1, Page and Elfer (2013) have pointed out the increasing recognition that working with young children places an emotional burden on the educator who requires resilience to build relationships with children, parents and colleagues and to work effectively with everyone. An essential element of this emotional requirement is compassion, both for the children but also importantly for one's own well-being.

Early years work requires both stability-within-self and the capacity to respond flexibly to the changing needs/wishes/emotions of others.

(Georgeson and Campbell-Barr, 2015, p 330).

Taggart (2014) further argues that compassion in early years teaching is an ethical requirement. The importance of the child as an individual is paramount, and the educator's care is essential to enable each child to achieve their full potential. It enables the child's views to be heard and taken into account. The United Nations Convention on Human Rights (1989) established that even the youngest children have the right to a voice, and Morgan (2014) reported that the majority of children in his survey felt that their rights were being respected. As Taggart states, *'Compassionate pedagogy seeks to nurture children who are vocal, capable citizens as well as secure, well-adjusted people'* (2014, p 173). Bearing this in mind, what values do you want the children to develop? Is it possible to develop values if you don't understand your own?

Reflection

» How does compassion fit into your values and beliefs about your role as an educator?

» Do you see it as a fundamental aspect of your role?

» Are you compassionate towards yourself? Compassion towards oneself is a pre-requisite for being compassionate towards others.

How can you support students to recognise compassion?

It is likely that most students and professionals would tend to think of themselves as being compassionate and would see this as a central motivation in their work. This is reflected in the articles noted in Chapter 1 about the prevalence of an ethic of care as expressed by those working in the early years. However, how much real attention is paid in day-to-day practice to needs of children and how are they expressed? As an educator, guiding a student into early years practice offers its own challenges.

Reflection

How would you support a student to respond in the following scenario?

A four-year-old child starts in a class half-way through a term and comes into school every morning and takes his shoes off. He slides along the corridor with great glee, but if asked to put his shoes back on will only do so after repeated requests, and sometimes hides his shoes and explains he can't find them. When the teacher insists he puts his shoes on, the boy becomes tearful. The headteacher has noticed the occasional lack of shoes in assembly, and the classroom assistant reports that the boy's new friends have begun taking their shoes off too.

» How should the student react?
» Who do they need to talk to?
» What are the key issues here – on behalf of the boy and on behalf of the school?

The educator needs to identify their own stance in order to be an effective advocate for quality. They need to be able to articulate their decisions to others in a supportive and understandable way if they are to be effective. What does the

UN Convention on the Rights of the Child (www.unicef.org.uk/what-we-do/un-convention-child-rights) have to say about educational practice in England? Are the longer-term *'needs of the child'* however perceived (eg school readiness) more of a guidance than day-to-day needs? How do we, for example, implement *'the rights and responsibilities of parents and carers to provide guidance and direction to their child as they grow up, so that they fully enjoy their rights?'* This must be done in a way that recognises the child's increasing capacity to make their own choices.

Conflicting standpoints

As an educator you may be confident about your own beliefs and values, and enjoy offering your students options about their growing understanding of their role, and the underpinning beliefs that they are starting to form, or which they may have formed before they began. However each of our roles is nested within a much wider set of professional relationships and others with whom we or our students come into professional contact with may not necessarily share the same set of values. This can pose challenges for all concerned In the early years; this is frequently manifest at the transitional points between different setting contexts and even within the same setting between professionals working in other age phases and in other roles. It may be necessary for example to ask our students to reflect on how well their beliefs and values align with those of colleagues who teach babies and younger children? Or conversely, how do their views about leadership, and potentially compassionate practice align with those in Key Stage 1 (KS1) and KS2?

Reflection

Challenging behaviour: Alisa is four years old and has just started school. She is the youngest child in her family, and the only girl. She finds it difficult to share with other children, and always refuses if another child wants to engage in an activity with her, becoming quite aggressive towards them. In the last few days, she has started biting children who approach her, causing considerable distress for the children (and their parents), and increasing her isolation in the class.

» How would you advise a student to deal with the situation?

» Is this an issue about behaviour management, or is it an indication of Special Educational Needs and Disabilities (SEND)?

» How might the student approach Alisa's parents, and the parents of the children who have been bitten?

IN A **NUTSHELL**

The educator's beliefs, values and ethical stance provide strong underpinnings for their practice and interactions with young children. Understanding your own beliefs and values, and their justifications is essential if you are to have a clear and sustainable vision for your practice, which can be shared with students and professionals you are working with.

As educators, we often share good and effective practice which helps to improve and sustain it. In the same way, exploring your beliefs and values with others enables you to clarify and strengthen them, and strongly supports your professional development.

REFLECTIONS ON **CRITICAL ISSUES**

In this chapter we have examined the importance of values, beliefs and an ethical approach in early years education, emphasising the importance of the educator assessing and understanding their own perspective. We have examined the terminology and its use, and exhorted the reader to engage in an evaluation of their own views. We have sought to demonstrate how this underpins practice, and how important it is in effective team working, successful leadership and in offering guidance to students.

We have alluded to some of the theories that have helped to shape practice in the early years. We have also considered the growing emphasis on compassion in early years education, both in practice and for the educator as an individual. At the heart of the argument has to be the child, and what is best practice if each child is to achieve their potential.

Further reading

Palaiologou, I (2012) *Ethical Practice in Early Childhood*. London: Sage.

Rees, T (2018) *Wholesome Leadership: the Heart, Head, Hands and Health of School Leaders*. Woodbridge: John Catt Education.

Values Education Trust (Vb-E) is an excellent resource for practising teachers. Available at: www.valuesbasededucation.com

CHAPTER 4 | THE LEARNING RELATIONSHIP: PRINCIPLES OF EFFECTIVE LEARNING AND PRACTICE IN THE EARLY YEARS

Gillian Lake

CRITICAL ISSUES

- *What are the key learning relationships?*
- *How can they be implemented and evaluated?*
- *How do we know that learning relationships are effective?*

Introduction

This chapter will present a model of learning that focuses on the interactions and transactions between children and adults and their learning environments. The chapter will follow up on the ideas about effective teaching and learning and developmentally informed practice in the early years introduced in Chapter 3. As with the philosophical ideas presented in Chapter 3, readers will be given parameters and guidance for how they can sift various forms of evidence and reach informed decisions.

Defining a learning relationship

Historically, definitions of learning relationships have tended to include the child and the teacher only. This traditional view of teaching has been challenged and the relationship has been widened to other participants. For interactionist writers such as Vygotsky (1978), knowledge is seen as a negotiated human construct. It is not something that exists to be consumed. There is a joint construction of meaning, a so-called *co-construction*, as the child *interacts* with others to learn about the world. Sameroff (2009) argues that when children are learning, interaction is not simply *interaction* but a *transaction* where one party (usually the child) is changed by the actions of the other. He challenged the interactionist perspective and theorists, such as Vygotsky, for making the assumption that interaction can occur between the child and another, namely the adult, during which both parties remain constant over time. He does not maintain that the relationship is unidirectional with the child acting on his environment, or the environment influencing the child. Rather, it is a bidirectional relationship, where both the environment and the child have an influence on each other. His theory suggests that the child, whom he terms the '*phenotype*', has a transaction with the '*environotype*', who are the peers, family and anyone in the cultural environment who can, potentially, socialise the child. He likens the environotype to Bronfenbrenner's mesosystem (Bronfenbrenner, 1979). This environotype influences the child through interaction over his/her lifetime and not just as a snapshot in time. The environotype also has the responsibility for regulation of the child, so that the child can become an adult. It is an *'organisational framework'* (Sameroff, 2009, p 15).

Learning and acquisition of knowledge then is a dynamic process involving many other key parties, such as:

- the teacher;
- other children;
- parents;
- other key adults in the children's lives at school, at home and in their wider environment.

Students need to obtain the skills to incorporate these key players into their teaching practice, in order to facilitate an environment for children, where optimum learning can take place. A sense of fun in learning can also help to develop the learning relationship between the teacher and the children and the children and each other. Teacher educators can support students in this endeavour through enabling peer-to-peer collaboration.

Reflection

Consider the following idea for a workshop with students.

Workshop on the theme of Physical development

Students had received a lecture on the theoretical underpinnings previous to the workshop, and were encouraged to put that theory into practice and teach each other to juggle. The learning outcome of the activity was to facilitate the students' reflection on the theory, ie the parts of the body required to learn such a new skill, but also the interactions they had with their classmates and the lecturer. They were given instructions and had to guide their partners in relation to these instructions. They may have had to adapt the instructions depending on the level of ability of their partner. They may have had to demonstrate and/ or coach their partner. They had to pay special attention to the differentiation in the room and the many differing abilities among their classmates. The students were given time at the end of the session to reflect on the activity. They used Gibb's model of reflection (1988). This helped them to reflect on their role as the teacher in the facilitation of the learning relationship between their classmates and themselves, and how they reacted to various aspects of the task and to each other.

- » As an educator, what key messages would you highlight to students from this type of activity?
- » How would you do so in a way that opened up a discussion rather than simply telling students what to look for?
- » Could you use such an approach for other aspects of training? Perhaps you could draft some ideas and share with colleagues who might also be working with you on various courses.

Children as collaborators in the learning relationship

Young children can share goals and play together; this ability to take a role each enables children to play collaboratively. Siraj-Blatchford (2009) maintains that peer play, in particular, is important for children around the age of four years. This is, she contends, when children can develop reciprocal and collaborative play. This, in turn, facilitates interaction where learning can follow. Adults, including students and trainees, should not be preoccupied with simply transmitting knowledge, but with creating a stimulating environment where a child's learning can take place, ie as an enabler. Child-initiated play can provide a context for this type of learning to take place.

The student or trainee's role in child-initiated collaborative activities

Howard (2010) highlights the crucial role of the adult in children's play. She maintains that adults should strive to be accepted as play partners by children. This might mean understanding the theoretical underpinnings of play, so that practitioners can approach tasks playfully. Increasing students' understanding of play may encourage their interaction with, and indeed their instruction through, play with children. Smilansky's (1968) teacher continuum could be used to inform trainees of how to develop a playful approach in their practice with young children.

Smilansky's (1968) model suggests that the adults' role might include:

- » *Visually looking on, where he/she encourages the children to play out a variety of roles and situations using language, and stands by to assist if needed;*
- » *Offering non-directive statements such as:* I see you have the pots and pans;

» *Posing questions to encourage the child to use the appropriate language, such as:* now you have the pots and pans, what will you do with them and what will you say?

» *Using directive statements, by deciding what roles the children will play, or by directing where the play goes next;*

» *Modelling the appropriate language or actions themselves, by using a prop.*

Research has shown that the adult is an integral aspect of children's play and that the majority of young children actually defined play as having a practitioner or teacher present (Howard, 2010). This, however, may not be the case for all children. Students need to be able to act reflexively when interacting with children through play, to adapt their approach, depending on individual children's needs or preferences.

There can be tension between the pedagogical frameworks surrounding play, on the one hand, and policies to which teachers, practitioners and students adhere, on the other. This results in recommendations for practitioners that are ambiguous (Wood, 2010). As a result, work–play dichotomies exist, which can result in children being left to play in non-interactive ways with adults, and play being viewed as something that does not underpin learning.

Furthermore, when adults approach children's play, they can receive an unwelcoming reaction from young children, as they are not always used to playing alongside adults. This can result in a reluctance on the part of students to interfere in children's play. However, in Howard's study, young children were found to have a broad perception of play, which *included* the presence of a teacher. When it comes to younger children, then, students have a responsibility to approach play, join in and set up precursors through story, in order to be accepted as play partners. Increasing the understanding of play can simultaneously empower students and allow children to be creative. Pushing the boundaries in teacher education can be beneficial with regard to the role of the adult. For example, workshops could simulate early years classrooms and small group instruction, so students can experience what young children experience. Instructors could employ early years playful pedagogies such as socio-dramatic play in the teaching of their own module content, so trainees can see best practice modelled.

The student or trainee's role as a direct instructor in small groups

Small group instruction can also provide opportunities for children to interact directly with the practitioner or student. Both the student and child can answer and ask very specific questions related to the lesson content. Opportunities arise for conversations to occur and for each child to be able to contribute to the discussion at his/her level.

Children's responses may vary across the age-range in the early years. Babies and toddlers, who have not yet learned how to fully verbalise their needs and responses, may rely on non-verbal communication strategies along with vocalisations. Students need then to become accustomed to the careful scrutiny of young children's responses during small group instruction. Such young children may not have developed the skills to work in a group. These children may require one-to-one attention. Due time and consideration has to be given to all children in the group, so children feel that they are all valuable contributors, no matter how they engage or respond. Students need to experience working one-to-one, or in small groups, with all ages in the early years cohort while on placement. This can help students to identify and practise strategies that increase young children's engagement in learning. Such a strategy might include starting from the child's own interests.

Starting from the child in the learning relationship

Bruner et al (1976) argued that the best context for the development of the learning relationship was from the child's own interests and/or experiences. Children use their own previous experiences on which to build new knowledge. Fisher (2013) echoed this viewpoint, emphasising the importance of working with young children on authentic tasks in meaningful contexts, rather than delivering abstract instruction, which is out of context for them. Students can provide learning environments that mirror real-world settings. While students can learn to cater to children's interests and agency in relation to their learning, a balance needs to be struck between the rights of the individual child to pursue their own interests and the needs of the overall group. Students can be guided to manage this by allowing children to express their creativity in certain tasks, while adhering to the wider curricular content. An equitable approach to including the children's interests can be encouraged. Fisher (2013) argued that starting with the children's interests is the key to unlocking their motivation and ultimately their learning.

Dweck (1999) contends that motivational processes influence the child's acquisition, transfer and use of knowledge and skills. If the child is extrinsically motivated, the motivation is coming from outside the child. For example, the child may be reacting to reward systems imposed on him/her in the classroom. This level of support usually fails to support children's actual learning needs and can lead to disaffection. However, if the child is intrinsically motivated, levels of interest and perseverance are increased and learning is optimised as a result. This can lead to increased well-being in the child, which can develop children's self-efficacy. This can all have a positive effect on his/her learning (Dweck, 1999).

Students need to be able to recognise motivation patterns of young learners. This ensures that they can identify when children do not wish to participate, do not understand or have a more general need. Teacher educators need to encourage students to pay close attention to children's interaction with other children and the materials that they encounter in the setting. These behaviours can act as signifiers to the student as to the overall level of engagement of, and learning opportunities taken by, the children. This can take the format, for students, of more formalised age-appropriate assessment practices, in order to ascertain whether their instruction has been effective.

Reflection

» How will you enable students to distinguish when particular strategies are/are not appropriate?

» Do you think students and professionals are likely to be comfortable in all the potential contexts they encounter? If not, how can you help them to become more open to different learning contexts?

» How will you ensure that students are aware of the need to be responsive to all of the children and yet to balance the needs of the whole group?

» You might also reflect on how each of these questions relates to how you will work with the different students in your groups.

Assessment of the effectiveness of the learning relationship

Effective teaching can be broken down into three constituent parts, ie planning for children's learning, supporting children's learning and reviewing children's learning or assessment. Reviewing children's learning creates the opportunity to both provide insight into students' and trainees' own effectiveness, and shine a light on the children's thinking and learning (Drummond, 2012).

Modes of assessment of children's learning

Standardised testing

Summative standardised assessment or classroom testing can be an effective way for assessing knowledge gained in relation to certain criteria in test conditions. Standardised testing is used widely in research and has been useful in this regard (Sammons et al, 2008). The results from such studies have informed policy shifts and furthered the case of early learning. These tests have rigorous norm-referencing to ensure they are reliable and valid. However, in the early years classroom contexts, standardised tests can omit other relevant strengths of the young child. Students need to learn to question what they specifically wish to assess and then make a reasoned judgement about which form of assessment to use. For example, students may wish to investigate a more holistic depiction of the young child. Here they may need to consider:

» skill development;
» stimulation/motivation;

- » security;
- » talk;
- » multi-sensory responses;
- » achievement;
- » practice and perseverance;
- » understanding;
- » feedback;
- » variety and diversity.

These dimensions may call for a more formative approach to assessment. This encompasses many different assessment methods for learning. One of these, the most pervasive and useful assessment technique in the early years – observation – will be discussed here.

Observation

Observations of individual children in the early years are much more manageable in a small group. It can be challenging for practitioners to find the time in large groups – when the needs of so many children are so diverse – to assess and observe children fully (Drummond, 2012). The small group affords the practitioner the time to observe and interact with the child for longer periods and obtain a more reliable assessment of the child's holistic ability. One strategy for documenting the small group observations of children's learning is through the use of *learning stories.*

Learning stories

A learning story is a snapshot in time relating to an observation of a child or small group of young children (Carr and Lee, 2012). Learning stories can make the *thinking,* and the interactions associated with that thinking, visible. It is worth noting that like standardised testing, learning stories cannot present a full and holistic picture of the child's learning, as they are only a snapshot and may not take place often enough. However, their beneficial use in relation to capturing the strengths of the child are discussed here. Figure 4.1 might be a useful way of conveying the learning story cycle to students.

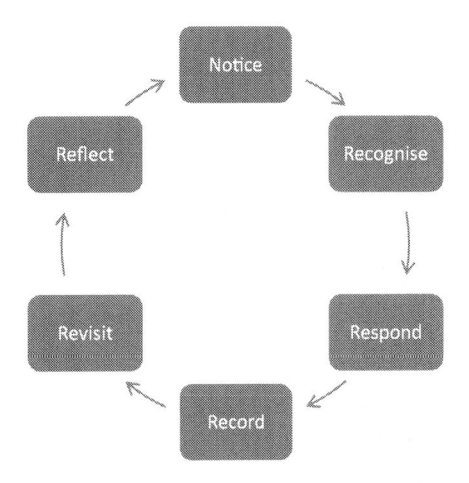

Figure 4.1 Learning story (Carr and Lee, 2012).

Crucially the assessment process begins with a student noticing a child's interest. Students might recognise this as a learning opportunity to be observed and begin observing the child. They may be active participants in the observation, or simply respond by providing a problem or resources for the child to use, to pursue this interest. Then they begin to record what they see. Students may record after the event, or take notes while it occurs. Either way, the student will be finalising their write-up after the learning activity.

Teacher educators can coach students in writing these observations using the following starting points.

» Use photographs as a starting point (if the students have permission to take photographs of the learning episode). Students should describe the photograph in relation to the learning that was taking place, rather than only offering a caption for it.

» Use subjective, rich language in the description of the event. Educators can provide examples of photographs or video footage already present in the school to facilitate students' practice of this.

» Write in the first person to ensure their voice is a strong presence in the record.

» Focus on the positive attributes of the learning episode and what the child can do rather than what they have failed to do.

After the student has described the event, they must then record the significance of it in relation to the child's learning. This may be directly related to the learning goals, skills and dispositions in the Early Years Foundation Stage and may even be subject-specific. Educators can support students by discussing the events in relation to the curricular frameworks and teaching standards.

An ideal time to practise the use of learning stories is when students are in the classroom on practical placements. Students can focus on four or five target children over the course of a month during their placement and complete learning stories for these individual children. Educators can scaffold and support students in developing skills, which they will go on to use when teaching independently.

This type of documentation of assessment is one area where students can develop skills for working in partnership with another of the key players in the learning relationship: parents. Parents are offered a blank page in which to respond to the story. This may be an anecdote regarding the child engaging in a similar activity in the home learning environment. Or they may choose to simply respond to the learning activity as presented from the setting. Educators can facilitate the interpretation of parents' responses and support the student in using the information for future discussions with parents. Educators may be present during these discussions and offer feedback to students regarding their approach to future learning for the child. What should be emphasised during the process to students is that the parents' contributions are valid, useful and an integral part of a wider learning relationship.

Parental engagement

Children's development can be supported by parents and practitioners working in partnership (Evangelou et al, 2008). Feelings of security and acceptance are enhanced as children observe warm relationships between their family and setting staff. This supports children's developing social skills and strengthens connections to their culture and sense of identity. Reynolds and Clements (2005) suggest that partnership between settings and parents should encompass any interaction on behalf of children, along with parents' participation as active partners in their child's education. They argue for recognition from practitioners that parents are a primary influence on their children's lives.

From the parents' perspective also, research suggests that parents seek to have their views taken into account by the setting (Fitzpatrick, 2012). But there are challenges associated with active engagement of parents in the learning relationship.

The main challenge is time. This is a factor that challenges all parties. For example, parents are often constrained by work commitments and their engagement can be limited as a result. Time constraints can also provide a challenge for staff with the pressures of fulfilment of curricula and paperwork.

Parental engagement can also be limited by socio-economic factors. Parents may be experiencing lower confidence as a result of limited educational opportunities. Confidence is a theme that is mirrored in staff experiences too. Staff often cite a lack of confidence about their own professional expertise as a mitigating factor in how they engage with parents. Part of this could be related to the minimal preparation they receive for the role. Ward (2018) argues that opportunities for interaction with parents should become an integral feature of placement for pre-service practitioners. In addition, she recommends, the facilitation of pre-service and in-service practitioners' reflection on the practitioner–parent relationship (Ward, 2018).

Promoting parental engagement

Epstein's (2001) model could be used by educators to prepare students in relation to the promotion and facilitation of parental partnership. The model suggests six elements.

1. *Parenting*: Support parents to create home learning environments, which support *children as learners* in the home.
2. *Volunteering*: Recruit parents to help at various stages in the school day/year with activities in the school or trips out.
3. *Communicating*: Establish robust and frequent two-way communication systems to track the child's development and progress in all areas.
4. *Learning at home*: Offer information that might support parents' attempts to learn with their child at home, eg booklists.
5. *Decision-making*: Ensure that parents are actively involved in policy and strategic decisions that are made in the setting in relation to the child's learning.
6. *Collaboration with the community*: Recognise and use resources from within the child's community to enrich the curriculum in the setting, eg cultural or social practices or community health (Epstein, 2001).

Parental involvement needs to reflect the diversity of families in communities. This will be addressed in more detail in Chapter 5. However it is worth noting here the valuable, and often overlooked, contribution that fathers can make to the learning environment. The Department of Health in Australia (2014) has recommended several ways in which to further engage fathers. The report suggests that students could:

- observe how often they specifically involve fathers;
- involve fathers in policy planning or setting development;
- develop father-friendly activities, such as social events;
- provide an approachable atmosphere at the setting;
- reference the positive role of fathers in setting publications; and
- use the father as a first point of contact in communicating with parents.

Practitioners have a responsibility to empower parents in the belief that their contribution is valid, valued and necessary. It can be difficult and challenging. A knowledge–power tension can exist in practitioner–parent relationships. Generally, setting managers do strive to give parents an active voice in their child's education, while not compromising the practitioners' professional status. Some students will go on to eventually manage settings themselves. It is essential that they are given the knowledge and skills to engage parents as partners.

Educators can positively promote the parental role and provide strategies for their students that will enable the involvement of parents in the management of the setting. This might include:

- » ensuring that parents have read and understood the setting's policies and procedures;
- » involving parents in the design, ratification, review and updating of those policies;
- » inviting parents to be collaborators, rather than consumers of educational experiences in the setting.

Parental involvement is a cornerstone of the learning relationship and the students' adequate preparation for this aspect of it is essential. They need to develop the skills to recognise when this relationship is functioning effectively, and when it needs to adapt different or new pathways.

Reflection

- » What sort of feedback from educators might help students to develop their confidence in the evaluation of their interaction with parents?
- » How can educators structure their programmes to include opportunities for students to engage directly and formally with parents?
- » How can educators best advise students to respond to the variety of informal feedback, positive and negative, that they may receive from parents?
- » How can we advise students to reach out to parents who may be less forthcoming than others?

The importance of care in the learning relationship

Contact with young children can be all encompassing and the implications in terms of '*emotional labour*' for students and professionals were discussed in Chapter 1. In relation to the learning relationship in practice, the Key Person system in England means that practitioners are explicitly required to develop interactions with young children (Department for Education, 2017). Practitioners need to

ensure that every child's care is tailored to meet their individual needs to help the child become familiar with the setting, offer a settled relationship for the child and build a relationship with their parents.

(Department for Education, 2017, p 22)

When a young child is new to the setting he/she will look for familiarity so as to feel comfortable in the new environment. This helps him/her to gain a foothold and ultimately increases his/her self-esteem. This can be challenging when staff are working part-time and the child is attending full-time, or vice-versa. The key person may not be present for key moments. In this scenario, it is imperative that there are procedures for when the key person is absent. As it is possible for a child to attach to many key people (Ainsworth et al, 1978), the child can be introduced to an alternative or substitute key person who can support that child.

The key person will be expected to maintain a professional distance while still enabling an attachment to occur. This balance can be a challenge for new or early career practitioners. Students need adequate training for addressing the particular circumstances they are facing. For example, if the child has additional needs, it behoves the management of a setting to provide information, support, ongoing guidance and strategies for the practitioner for the management and learning relationship with the child on a day-to-day basis. Professional dialogue has a key role to play in this. Strategies can be discussed and experiences can be shared with colleagues. Professional dialogue with professionals outside of early years is helpful and necessary in some cases. Access to parenting charities, psychological services, social workers and other key professionals on a regular basis can help the student to reflect on, and obtain knowledge on, best practice. This facilitates a more holistic approach to the development of the learning relationship with the child and indeed supports the trainee's own emotional well-being.

Reflection

» Consider how you view the multiple learning relationships so far discussed. How can you accord each equal significance?

» Is this possible or desirable? Why do you think that?

» Can you foresee any tension between different layers of relationships?

» Which aspect of each of these learning relationships do you think students might find most challenging and how could you build in opportunities to have professional dialogue around these matters?

The influence of policy on the development of the learning relationship

As noted in Chapter 1, a body of evidence has been growing internationally that has been concerned with the increasing regulation of early education and care (Urban, 2015). This regulation has taken the form of increased accountability linked to an emphasis on quality (Sammons et al, 2008). It is hard to dispute an emphasis on quality outright, due to the benefits that might have for young children. However, if this emphasis is coupled with stringent measures of accountability in relation to children's academic outcomes, then this can affect the staff who are interacting with young children. The pressure to assess and complete profiles can reduce both the spontaneity and creativity of trainees' teaching and the time spent interacting with young children.

Baseline assessment

One particular measure of accountability that was introduced by the UK government (at the time of publication in 2016) and subsequently opened up as a saleable product to the private sector innovation labs was baseline testing of young children. When it was first introduced, it was mandatory for settings to engage in it. Following pressure from early years lobby groups, this subsequently changed to suggested best practice (Roberts-Holmes and Bradbury, 2017). Assessment of young children using analytical tools has become a criterion for success in inspection reports and can dictate parental preferences. However, some commentators have remarked that such baseline testing can be problematic, as it reduces early education and care to an economic commodity. Early education can be used to achieve government targets on social mobility, as the child is tracked throughout his/her schooling. Baseline tests have been regarded as being quite reductionist, as they usually measure children's development in a number of curricular areas with only two options, ie whether the child has reached a particular milestone or not. Some children may not meet that particular milestone at all, and some children are very near meeting it, ie the very next day. In these cases, the children's development and learning is being represented inaccurately by a single time point. This is particularly pertinent in the increasingly diverse context within which English early years settings operate (Moss, 2014). All children cannot be uniformly assessed in this way. For example, it is not always appropriate, or suitable, to assess children with additional needs in this way.

Baseline assessment attempts to reduce young children's complex learning to a single number, thus representing extreme educational reductionism. Baseline can be understood as *'nothing but a ridiculous simplification of knowledge and a robbing of meaning from individual histories'* (Malaguzzi, from Cagliari et al, 2016, p 378) and therefore stands in contrast to socio-cultural theory, which has demonstrated that children learn within and through sets of social relationships. Therefore, it is crucial that students have an awareness of the limitations of such assessment techniques, which contrast with the now accepted theoretical foundations of interactional learning. Ongoing professional dialogue with a particular focus on the critical awareness of the suitability of such assessments, with regard to children's individual and diverse needs, would enable students to consider the whole child's development.

More broadly there is an increase in data production, following an overall trend for the expansion of data and accountability agendas in society more generally (Roberts-Holmes and Bradbury, 2016). Students need to be introduced to the ethical, moral and indeed pedagogical debate surrounding the management and collection of such data. It is the responsibility of the teacher educator to empower the student to question what they are being asked to adopt in relation to their practice in the future. Placing an emphasis on development of students' critical thinking skills in relation to the effectiveness of pedagogy might address this to some extent.

Developing critical awareness and evidence-based approach to practice

With the widening possibilities for access to first-hand research about the early years, with avenues such as open access journals, social media and news websites, it can be challenging for students to assimilate all the information on offer. Chapter 6 will address this issue in detail. This section will meanwhile focus on some ideas to support the development of students' critical thinking skills in order to enable them to develop an evidence-based approach to practice. This includes an analytical appreciation of the conclusions an author or researcher is making and whether these are justified, based on the methodology that was employed. This does not mean that students need to have an in-depth knowledge of the intricate details of research or analysis methods, but an overall appreciation for when research has been carefully and robustly carried out would be helpful. Some key aspects of rigorous research might be:

» the suitability of the methodology used in relation to the research question posed;
» the participants, ie in a quantitative study, whether the sample size is sufficient to be seen as representative and in a qualitative study whether the participants' views are accurately represented;
» the generalisability of the context of the research;
» the presence of any bias and how this might have been addressed.

Professional dialogue with colleagues and between students and educators can offer the opportunity to discuss evidence in this critically aware manner. Engaging in meaningful and challenging conversation with experienced peers about the often-contradictory research evidence can enhance students' appreciation, understanding and critiquing of the learning relationship. This practice has the potential to increase students' personal and professional confidence to question policy decisions relating to their development as competent and caring early years professionals.

IN A **NUTSHELL**

The learning relationship is an organic ever-changing relationship that depends on the key players that constitute it. When working together, parents, other adults, other children and the child can develop a rich, diverse and caring learning relationship. The evaluation of this relationship is central to its success. Age-appropriate methods of assessment must be considered seriously if this relationship is to keep evolving and developing.

> ### REFLECTIONS ON **CRITICAL ISSUES**
> This chapter has examined the importance of the learning relationship for children's development. It has put the child at the centre, underscoring his/her agency in relation to his/her learning needs, and has highlighted the centrality of interactions between the adult and the child to respond to those needs. It has also emphasised the importance of developing real and practical relationships with parents. It has provided guidance on the appraisal of these relationships in relation to the wide-ranging, and sometimes contradictory, evidence that is available to students. It has positioned professional dialogue at the centre of the challenges covered, accentuating the positive effects it can have on students' developing practice.

Further reading

Fisher, J (2013) *Starting from the Child: Teaching and Learning in the Foundation Stage*. Maidenhead: Open University Press.

Gibbs, G (1988) *Learning by Doing: A Guide to Teaching and Learning Methods*. Oxford: Oxford Further Education Unit.

Smilansky, S (1968) *The Effects of Sociodramatic Play on Disadvantaged Preschool Children*. New York: John Wiley & Sons.

Vygotsky, L (1978) in Cole, M, John-Steiner, V, Scribner, S and Souberman, E (eds) *Mind in Society: The Development of Higher Psychological Processes*. Cambridge, MA: Harvard University Press.

CHAPTER 5 | UNDERSTANDING THE FAMILY AND CULTURAL CONTEXTS FOR LEARNING

Catharine Gilson

CRITICAL **ISSUES**

- Why is it important for early years students and professionals to establish a relationship with the families of the children they teach?
- What do educators need to take into consideration in order to understand the family as a cultural context for learning?
- How can early years students and professionals work constructively with families and the wider community so as best to support young children?

Introduction

This chapter will consider the wider contexts in which children learn, and focus in particular on the significance of the relationships between students and professionals and the families of the young children they teach. The UK has a long history of promoting the notion of teachers working in partnership with parents or carers of the children in their school as Cottle and Alexander (2014) point out in their seminal study. However, it is first helpful to try to define what the term *family* is taken to mean in the context of today's society. It is also useful to ask why it is regarded as important that the adults involved in young children's learning should work together and form positive relationships. In the section that follows both these questions are addressed and the main discourses or ways of framing the relationship between home and school are outlined.

Why is it important for early years professionals to establish a relationship with the families of the children they teach?

The family is a tricky concept to define in such a way so as to include the multiplicity of forms that it can take. The UK Office of National Statistics (ONS) provides the following definition:

A family is a married, civil partnered or cohabiting couple with or without children, or a lone parent, with at least one child, who live at the same address. Children may be dependent or non-dependent.

(ONS, 2018)

However, as Street and Wild (2013) point out, it is questionable whether this definition encompasses other forms of family units such as the extended family, where several generations may live together, or the fluidity of some family structures, where children may move between parents who live apart, for example. Nonetheless, if one takes the family of the child to include the parents or caregivers responsible for the child, then it is worth thinking for a moment about why teachers are encouraged to work in partnership with them. One powerful reason is the importance of the home learning environment for the outcomes of children, as discussed in the previous chapter. However, working in partnership with parents and caregivers depends above all on making and sustaining positive relationships with the adults who are bringing up the children we teach in our schools and settings. The holistic nature of the teaching and learning relationship with young children is emphasised by Brooker (2010) and includes parents and communities as integral elements. Brooker sees the pedagogic relationship in early childhood education as triangular, with both practitioner and parent involved in supporting the child, and, it could be argued, supporting each other in their joint endeavour to work together in the best interests of the child. This is a particularly pertinent model for those working in early childhood education where the children are still very young, often not fully articulate and are dependent to a large extent on their parents and on the other adults who care for them to interpret and respond to their needs.

It is easy to forget what Youell (2006) terms '*the leap of faith*' that parents have to make when they entrust their young and child or baby to the care of a relative stranger in a school or nursery setting. This is especially challenging too for a teacher faced with a class of 30 children to get to know, as well as their families. The challenge of establishing trusting and mutually respectful relationships with parents and caregivers, particularly at the start of the children's more formal school life, is rarely acknowledged in policy or practice but should not be underestimated. The vignette below is a reminder of how emotional and fragile the relationship can be, and how easily trust can be lost. This parent was very involved in her child's school and very keen to provide the best learning environment possible at home to support her daughter, but felt excluded from doing so by the lack of constructive feedback from her daughter's teacher at a parent's evening.

Case study

Extract from a research interview with a parent about her experience of her daughter's early years (nursery class and reception year) education.

Parent: I was quite shocked. I remember being quite shocked with how Gemma [teacher] was feeding back, because she did the first one, and she said this is their book (they had like a learning book), this is their book, tell me about

Sophie. And it was as if she couldn't tell me enough about Sophie, and I thought but you teach her every day. And I suppose I put my professional hat on [...] I think it's quite hard, maybe because there's two professionals in this house and we are always sticking our professional hats on. And I remember feeling I could have done better than that. If I'd done that in my job, or interviewed like that, I'd be shot. And I was quite surprised because I was thinking but teachers are professional as well, why aren't they trained in that kind of, you know, you've got to understand the dynamics of the parents, and if the parents are asking those questions you've got to change your tactic of how you are answering.

Reflection

You may like to consider your responses to the vignette above and reflect on your own approach to working with parents.

» What aspects of working with parents do you enjoy? What aspects do you find challenging?

» Do you agree with this parent that there is a need to train students and professionals in how to relate to adults as well as children?

» What do you think are the key skills that a student or professional needs to work effectively with parents and the community?

Parents as first educators of their children or parents as 'deficient'?

Two competing discourses of how parents are viewed and positioned in education dominate the policy and research on early childhood education. On the one hand the parent is viewed as the first educator of the child, with unique knowledge of the child. On the other hand, the parent is also construed as a deficient educator who needs guidance from the professionals, who are the experts in this matter (Cottle and Alexander, 2014). With the increasing prominence of accountability and assessment throughout the education system in England, it could be argued that the discourse of the deficient and non-agentic parent is increasingly prevailing over the notion that parents bring their own valuable knowledge to the pedagogic relationship. As touched on in Chapter 4, Roberts-Holmes (2015) has drawn our attention to the '*datafication*' of early years education in the UK, and it is notable that within this phase, assessment points are proliferating. In England, for example, there are assessments at two years old, then the Foundation Stage Profile at the end of the Early Years Foundation Stage (EYFS) (DfE, 2017) and the introduction of baseline assessment in Year 1. Some argue that within this context, the role of parents has been instrumentalised: they are expected to help their children achieve the learning outcomes that the educational system has set without being involved in the discussions regarding these outcomes, or consulted on the forms of education they would like for their children. Thus, risk of school failure is increasingly framed as a deficiency of families, rather than of schools, education systems and policies that drive them. Paradoxically, the recognition of the importance of the earliest years of a child's life on their future outcomes, along with the significant influence of the home learning environment, has led to increased pressure being brought to bear on early years professionals to 'close the gap' between the poorest families and the most affluent. This in turn can result in Early Childhood Education and Care (ECEC) curricula being framed in terms of future gains rather than in terms of developmentally appropriate practice.

However, there is also a discourse emerging that challenges the instrumentalised role of parents as agents of the government's educational agenda, and aims to address the unequal balance of power between the school and the family. These counter-narratives highlight discourses of empowerment and often focus on social justice, foregrounding marginalised groups of parents such as some immigrants, and giving them voice to express their hopes and dreams for their children's education and lives. In the UK the pioneering work of Pen Green Children's Centre in involving parents in their children's learning exemplifies this approach (see suggestions for further reading) and could best be described as family-centric rather than school-centric (Knopf and Swick, 2007). Alongside this discourse is a greater awareness of the positioning of parents in relation to practitioners, and a questioning of the power dynamic in the relationship and the assumption that the teacher always knows best. In an interesting empirical study, Brooker (2010) looked at the imposition of practices on parents that they do not find helpful, in the name of '*best practice*', such as home visits, and calls for more dialogue between practitioners and parents.

Reflection

» A recent study by Ute Ward (2018, see Further Reading) suggests that teacher' attitudes towards working with parents change with their classroom experience, age and life experience.

» How might these factors influence the approach you take to training students who may have had a range of different experiences and be at different stages of their lives?

» Looking back at when you started teaching, what was the most useful advice you were given about working with parents, and what advice would you pass on to your students?

The picture that emerges is of a complex and at times contradictory relationship between families and schools, reflecting the debate in society of the role of parents in their children's education. It is also a highly emotional relationship for the parents at least, as seen in the earlier vignette, and one that is fragile, especially when children are young. Several researchers have commented on the rivalry that can arise between parents and teachers

(Youell, 2006; Salzberger-Wittenberg et al, 1983). This is potentially a particular issue in the early years, where, as Elfer (2012b) has pointed out, the misinterpretation of the Key Person Approach (KPA) can cause a blurring of boundaries between the parental and the professional role. In fact, Elfer argues that the theory behind the KPA conceptualises the role as distinct from the parental role, and complementary to it. This emphasis on recognising the difference of perspective between parents and practitioners is echoed in the next section, which looks at the family as a cultural context for learning.

What do educators need to take into consideration in order to understand the family as a cultural context for learning?

The notion of the family is an elusive concept to define, as acknowledged at the beginning of this chapter. This is even more the case when one considers the range of diversity that can be found within any community of the different types of families. Families may come from different ethnic, religious or linguistic backgrounds, for example, but the range is much more nuanced than that: they may be an immigrant family, a refugee family, asylum seekers or economic migrants for example. They may be of mixed race heritage and have lived in the UK for one generation or many generations. When one thinks of diversity in family life, as Knowles and Holmstrom (2013) point out, one has to include single-parent families, step families, re-constituted families, gay and lesbian families, families with a disabled child or parent, foster families and families with adopted children. Families are also dynamic entities, whose mode of functioning may change, due to such situations as bereavement, mental or physical illness, divorce and separation, unemployment and poverty. The range of potential diversity in any one class of children is immense, even when they all share the same language and ethnicity. Thus, establishing positive relationships to facilitate communication would seem to be beneficial to ensure the best outcomes for the child.

However, Vandenbroeck has a word of caution about the ways in which we as educationalists relate to families in a much cited editorial entitled '*Let Us Disagree*' (Vandenbroeck, 2009). Vandenbroeck acknowledges that there is generally a greater awareness of diversity in early childhood education now than 50 years ago, reflected in the shift of emphasis from assimilation to the dominant culture to a more inter-cultural approach. While he notes that there now appears to be an emerging consensus on the necessity to respect diversity and inclusion, he argues that this approach to diversity does not take account of what parents (or children) may want for their children's education. In many cases the parental aims may not coincide with what educationalists consider to be equitable and inclusive practice, but to ignore their wishes is to silence precisely the people that the education system wishes to engage. He observes that:

We have only begun to discuss with parents and children how to deal with issues of diversity in education, instead of deciding for them. What is also the case is that discussing these issues with them will entail many new disagreements on many new issues: language acquisition, the role of early childhood education in society, the multiple meanings of 'inclusion' or 'integration', the relationships between private and public spheres, the relationships between culture and religion etc.

(Vandenbroeck, 2009, p 167)

While Vandenbroeck acknowledges the complexity of the task that this presents early years professionals with, he contends that this difficult decision-making process in the face of divergent views is in fact what enables a practitioner and so, more broadly, a profession to reflect and develop:

Because it is precisely the disagreement that allows us to reflect about the decisions taken. There is nothing as deadly for a team as consensus. Indeed, in the daily practice of early childhood education, it is the exception, the odd question, the unexpected, the 'leakage' that raises the debates that makes professionalism 'progress'.

(Vandenbroeck, 2009, p 168)

Below, a parent shares her experiences of her youngest daughter, who started school shortly after they had arrived in England from Kenya.

Case study

Extract from a research interview with a parent talking about when her daughter started school.

Researcher: *Could you give me an example of being sensitive to cultural difference? You mentioned [an occasion with] your daughter where they weren't sensitive to her.*

Parent: *The first day she went to school they asked her to change in front of everybody. Being Muslim she couldn't so she cried and cried, and she came home and didn't want to go to that school anymore. And just that day I received a phone call from another school to which I had applied for as well, which was a little further from home, and said there's an availability; so I spoke to a friend and she said there are so many of our community there already so why don't you do that? So the first day I moved her out, she went to school and I moved her out. That, I felt, was something that could have helped her. And from day one, you know, first impression is a lasting impression, so whatever confidence she had she lost it in that one day.*

Reflection

» How might you discuss the vignette above with your students to consider how the situation could have been handled differently with both the child and the parent?

» Thinking of the families and children that you have worked with, and in particular the range of cultural diversity that you have experienced, are there examples from your practice that it would be useful to share with your students?

» How might you introduce your students to the tension in education between assimilating minority cultures into the dominant culture of a society and the notion of intercultural dialogue?

Notions of intercultural dialogue often involve the idea of negotiating a shared space between the different parties, rather than assimilating one culture into another. Cohen-Emerique (cited in Gibson and Street, 2013) talked of the '*culture shock*' that arises in everyday situations that has to be recognised in order for dialogue to take place. She identifies key areas of culture shock to include areas such as how different cultures view the human body (for example, how much is covered up or displayed, self-care practices), the different codes of social interaction (such as the level of eye contact, how people greet each other, personal space) and notions of family (what it comprises and the roles of those within it). Often religious beliefs influence cultural practices but it is also important to note that cultural practices may change from generation to generation, so what is the custom for the parents may not be the norm for their offspring.

In the vignette above, the shock experienced by the parent and her daughter is evident in the little girl's response when she was asked to change her clothes in front of other people, including boys, and her mother's response, which was to change her daughter's school to an environment where the family's religious beliefs and cultural practices regarding self-care would be treated more sensitively. In this case, it is possible to debate whether the sense of shock was so great that the parent did not attempt to have a conversation with the school, or whether the rules of social interaction where schools and teachers are respected, and not to be challenged, resulted in the parent changing her daughter's school rather than challenging the first school. To use a phrase borrowed from Cohen-Emerique, what we see in this vignette is an example of cultural dissonance.

The potential for cultural dissonance is perhaps greater than is often acknowledged in early years education and care in England, and impacts on some areas that are fundamental to our understandings of good practice. This is particularly the case for students and new teachers though it can also be experienced by established teachers. For example, attitudes to play vary widely from culture to culture (Keys Adair and Doucet, 2014) in terms of the role of toys and props, the role of the adults, the role of the environment and nature, the relationship of play to learning and the debate of whether play belongs at home or at school or in both places. Keys et al point out that in England, play and learning are more closely enmeshed than in other cultures, resulting in our notion of *educational play*, which is not shared by other cultures. In France, a key feature of play is that no adults should be involved; for example. Brooker (2005), in a study of a reception class, documents the culture shock experienced by two four-year-old Bengali boys when they start school, which instead of being formal, as their families have expected, involves playing with sand which is not only an alien activity but also one that in their cultural landscape has no place in a school. Brooker's findings suggest that the adjustment that these two little boys have to make to accommodate these conflicting cultural notions of what learning involves impact negatively on their engagement and hence their learning outcomes both during their reception year and subsequently.

Attitudes towards the place of the home language, if it is not the language of the host country, are similarly varied. In her study on young bilingual learners at home and at school, Drury (2007) illustrates this point with a case study of a mother and grandmother in a bilingual family, where both women saw the home as the place for the home language and culture and school as the place to learn English. They regarded home as the best place for the child before they started formal schooling, rather than other provision such as ECEC. All three mothers in the case studies reported by Drury had high educational aspirations for their daughters, but at the same time desired and expected their daughters to retain and develop their first language and culture. Yet this tension between wanting to retain a minority culture as well as achieve highly in the educational system in the dominant language is echoed in the EYFS, which calls for a child's culture and language to be respected, yet administers an assessment that requires children to function in English by the time they start Year 1. There are no easy answers to inter-cultural dialogue but these examples highlight our Anglo-centric attitudes to learning and remind us that as professionals in education, we know one way of teaching children, but it is not necessarily the only way. They call for us to approach our interactions with families with an open mind, ready to learn about not only their cultural context but also our own responses towards coping with difference and challenge.

How can early years educators work constructively with families and the wider community so as best to support young children?

The importance of working with families of young children to maximise their educational outcomes and so their life chances are emphasised by both the Field report (Field, 2010) and the Helping Parents to Parent report (Clarke and Younas, 2017) both of which focussed on improving social mobility. Clarke and Younas (2017), in their international review of parenting interventions, found that approaches based on empowerment and developing positive skills for parents seemed to be the most successful. They acknowledge that this is highly skilled work that is most effective when it is tailored to the specific needs of a local community. The notion of empowerment is premised on a relationship that is facilitative, supportive and collaborative. This principle is illustrated by the case study below, where a practitioner describes how she engages parents in the notion of outdoor learning.

Case study

Extract from a research interview with a practitioner, who is talking about how she enlists the support of parents for the Forest School visits that are an integral part of the school's early years curriculum.

Practitioner: *Parents come on the first visit. I personally quite like it; I don't feel nervous with the parents there. I kind of feel it's a privilege really to allow them to see what Forest School is about. Because before they didn't go, I used to go as the assistant, and the parents didn't go. So now, becoming the leader, I can help parents to see what a good thing it is, well I hope I can, to see what a good thing it is, and to share experiences. And also I found last week a parent did come to the woods for a second visit, because she was nervous about her child coming, again a parent from a different culture, and she explained to me why she felt so nervous about her child going. And I learnt something from that as well.*

Researcher: *Why did she feel so nervous?*

Practitioner: *For one she thought the wooded area was in a different place, she thought her child had to walk much further, she thought it was out in the open to the public, which it's not, and she just thought her child would be left to kind of, just to do nothing basically.*

Reflection

» What approach would you encourage your student to take to including parents in the learning environment indoors and/or outdoors?

» What are the potential benefits and challenges of welcoming parents into a school or nursery environment that you think it would be useful to discuss with your student?

» If all parents were not able to accompany the Forest School visit here, what alternative ways of sharing the experience with them, and also allaying their worries, might you suggest to the student?

While both parents and practitioners are almost always both committed to working in the best interests of the child at the centre of the relationship, their relationship with the child is essentially different and their perspectives of early childhood education reflect this divergence. This is illustrated by a father's comments on his daughter's nursery experience in a research interview:

I've listened to people talking about play and development, so a bit of that is familiar to me. So I understand all that, and support it, celebrate it, blah blah. But the key aspect is that when we get up in the morning she can't wait to get here, and when I come and pick her up, she doesn't really want to go home, you know, she's had a fantastic time.

This extract also highlights the tension between care and education, with the parent here emphasising that the most important thing for him is not the educational quality of his daughter's experience at nursery but that she is happy and loves going to nursery. However, as demonstrated in the first vignette in this chapter, some parents are very concerned about their child's educational progress, and perhaps the most important message to give to students is to approach each encounter with parents with an open mind and a professional attitude. Professionalism involves being trained in the skills needed for the job and there are some key interactions with parents that it is useful for all early years educators to develop the skills to manage. These interactions include establishing a rapport, greeting parents and exchanging information informally on an everyday basis, both of a practical and developmental nature, and communicating more formally, as when there is a review meeting, or a cause for concern. It is challenging to communicate difficult or negative information sensitively and in a way that is honest and constructive, and it behoves us as educators to prepare students adequately so that they can develop the skills to manage the complexity of the learning relationship with the families of the young children they teach.

The principles underpinning this study illustrate the approach recommended by Evangelou and Wild (2014, p 388), namely a *'bi-directional approach where both partners are valued for the contributions they make to children's development'*. The authors caution against conceptualising parents as deficient in their parenting, even when the school does not value how they parent, as parents have a depth of knowledge about their child that is unique. The bi-directional approach they advocate requires practitioners to see parents as an essential part of the pedagogic relationship rather than as an inconvenience, and to welcome their views. This calls for considerable self-awareness, a high degree of reflexivity and a willingness to listen and challenge one's own assumptions as well as those of students coming into the profession. This willingness to engage in a dialogue with families and colleagues will be ongoing and dynamic, not only because of the richness and individuality of each family as discussed earlier in this chapter, but also because recent research suggests that practitioners have very different responses to working with parents and that these change with experience and age.

Part of welcoming families and communities is about taking children out into the community as well as welcoming them into the school community, by home visiting, taking the children to the local services and landmarks and encouraging them to participate in the life of the community. We may look for inspiration in how to do this in the New Zealand curriculum, Te Whariki, which includes a strong focus on children learning about their local community and heritage from their earliest years. The curriculum uses the image of a woven mat to represent the way in which all strands of children's lives are brought together in the curriculum, including the bilingual heritage of Maori and English languages and philosophies of early childhood education.

This will not be a new idea for the teacher mentor, as the New Zealand Te Whariki curriculum is known for its innovative and holistic approach in early childhood education internationally. Rather, this sentence serves as a reminder to introduce the student to these ideas in a broader context, and make the point that the English (as well as Welsh and Scottish) EY curriculum draws on ideas from many other countries.

Reflection

» Thinking back to the idea of a negotiated shared space between the school and the family, are there any areas of contest that you can think of that pose a dilemma?

» For example, when meeting parents for the first time or greeting them on parents' evenings, how might a teacher resolve the shaking hands dilemma in a diverse cultural environment, where in certain religions it is not customary for males and females to have any physical contact, including shaking hands? Would you advise the student not to shake hands with any of the parents in the class? Or only those parents who might not find the practice acceptable?

» And how might you advise a student to proceed if she or he is from a minority culture that is different from the majority of parents, and who has different cultural customs (eg regarding eye contact or physical contact)?

IN A **NUTSHELL**

Working with families is an essential part of educating and caring for young children. It is complex and demanding work and requires a high level of self-awareness and reflection, along with a willingness to work with parents in a mutually respectful and collaborative way in order to foster the best interests of the child.

REFLECTIONS ON **CRITICAL ISSUES**

The evidence supporting the importance of working with families to support their children in the earliest years of their lives is compelling, yet the complexity and diversity of establishing mutually beneficial relationships with families and the wider community pose many challenges for the early years teacher. However, returning to the child, it is worth remembering that both practitioners and parents, however diverse and dissonant their views are, are both concerned to support the child as best they can. So if they can work together productively, then the teaching and learning relationship will offer much more coherent and constructive support to the child.

Further reading

Ward, U (2018) How Do Early Childhood Practitioners Define Professionalism in Their Interactions with Parents? *European Early Childhood Education Research Journal.* DOI: 10.1080/1350293X.2018.1442043

Whalley, M and Pen Green Centre team (1997) *Working with Parents.* London: Hodder and Stoughton.

Young, S and Street, A (2010) *Time to Play: The Development of Interculturally Sensitive Approaches to Creative Play in Children's Centres Serving Predominantly Muslim Communities.* Oxford: PEEPLE (www.peeple.org.uk).

CHAPTER 6 | THE INFORMED PRACTITIONER
Mary Briggs

CRITICAL **ISSUES**

- What does it mean to be an informed practitioner as an educator of students and professionals?
- Why is it important to be an informed practitioner?
- How do you use evidence-based practice in your teaching and support practitioners to work with evidence informed practice?

Introduction

The conversation below illustrates an aspect of being an informed practitioner. This early years educator questions a student practitioner about her understanding of the need to be an informed practitioner.

SP: *Why should we assess children in the early years if they are going to complete a baseline test in reception classes?*

T: *Assessment is much more than a test; you are making judgements about what children can do all the time you interact with them in the setting. These judgements then inform what you will plan for children to engage with next, the questions you will ask to extend their thinking and so on. Assessment allows you to plan for the individual, groups and whole cohorts building on what they already know and stimulating them to ensure progress in their learning.*

SP: *That sounds so complicated. Isn't there just a book I can follow?*

T: *It sounds complex but assessment will become an integral part of your practice as you gain experience and you try different ways of working. We will introduce you to the theoretical perspectives associated with assessment and we will as a group compare these with practice to help you become an informed practitioner.*

SP = student practitioner; T = early years educator

This chapter looks at two aspects of the informed practitioner.

1. How those teaching on early years courses work with their students to develop them as informed practitioners?
2. How do those working on early years courses as early years educators continue to develop themselves as informed practitioners as part of ongoing continuing professional development (CPD) and what might be some of the key issues and debates that early years educators need to explore?

What does it mean to be an informed practitioner?

Does this mean that you are always up-to-date with research in your field? The answer is partly yes; it is useful to be up-to-date with what is going on at the cutting edge of research. This can take time, which can be difficult to carve out of a busy schedule for those teaching early years students. Whilst you might be encouraging your students to read as much as possible you will know that that in itself is a challenge. So, developing your students to become informed practitioners and professionals is not just about reading. You want to develop their skills of critiquing the policy and practice advice they are given rather than potentially following without question.

In this section the sub-sections will take you through a number of different aspects of why practitioners need to be well informed.

The student as an informed practitioner

As an early years educator working with students who work or will work in the early years you will be encouraging your students to become informed practitioners. It may be a challenge to demonstrate the value of being informed to your students. They may see their role as to complete tasks from others without questioning. How do you demonstrate this value not just whilst the students are studying but as a sustained focus throughout their career? Once you have successfully conveyed the value of being informed it is essential to equip students with guidance that will help them to critically discern purpose, value and credibility from the plethora of information and sources that are available. Table 6.1 opposite may be a useful starting point for this, suggesting questions that can be asked of various source materials.

Table 6.1 Where are the sources of information that assist you and your students being informed?

Source	Location	Critical issues/questions to ask
News items	Television and radio	Why has this become newsworthy? Have things gone wrong with the policies and practices? How reliable are the sources cited?
	Newspapers in print or online	Who is the journalist? Are there changes being proposed to funding or policy? How reliable are the sources cited? Is it specifically educational such as the *Times Educational Supplement* (TES)?
Social media	Twitter	Who started the thread? Who is being retweeted? What is the author's stance on the issue? Professional background – is this clear?
	LinkedIn	Are the authors of the post members of a professional group?
	Blog posts	Is the author writing as an individual or part of a larger organisation? Whose is the agenda emphasised in each item?
Books	Library bookshops	Are these practical guidance books with ideas for practitioners? Or are they theoretical discussions of research in the field?
Journal articles	Professional journals	Which organisation sponsors the journal? Who is the intended readership?
	Research journals	Are the papers peer refereed? Who is on the editorial board? Does the journal cover international issues?

Source	Location	Critical issues/questions to ask
Policy documents	Websites – Gov.uk	When were consultations posted? What are the timescales for decisions about policy changes? Who was consulted? Who took a lead in the policy changes? Were changes discussed in parliament?
Conferences	Conference websites	Who is organising the conference? Are there vested interests? Who are the speakers and what is their affiliation? Is there open access to papers/talks? What is the focus of the conference?
	Conference literature	Where was the conference taking place? Is it sponsored by publishers or resource manufacturers? Is there open access to papers/talks? Is it something you might attend?

Reflection

» Using each source of information in the table above how will you work with your students to enable them to make informed decisions about the quality and reliability of what they read?

» How might you encourage your students to use a range of different types of sources including those that might seem *too theoretical* or offputting at first?

An early years educator reflected on her early days as an early years educator:

I wanted to enthuse my students to read the exciting theories I had come to know and love. However, I learnt that diving straight into theory switched many of the students off reading. I learnt that there were different ways to approach this process and still get them willing to read. Starting with what they had observed and then analysing using the theory worked better; it helped them see the theory in action enabling them to make connections and see the relevance. This basis also enabled us to discuss values in practice and where they originated.

The early years educator as an informed practitioner

As an early years educator you will want to model good practice by demonstrating the importance of being informed about current thinking, policy and practice. Initially you may find it helpful to revisit your thoughts about your values (Chapter 3) and how you have established these. You might also look again at the table at the beginning of this chapter about sources of information and begin to consider what influences your thinking.

The early years educators' role in developing student practitioners as informed practitioners

Enabling students to see the benefits of being an informed practitioner is not easy if their focus is on what they need to complete to pass the programme rather than thinking ahead to how they develop their career including considering leadership roles. (It would be worth returning to Chapter 2 here to consider how being an informed practitioner fits with professional identity.)

Reflection

» How do you adhere to your values whilst remaining open to new ideas?
» How do you respond to challenges from the students that what you are saying they don't see happening in practice?

Developing the idea of evidence-based practice

Evidence-based practice (EBP) is an interdisciplinary approach initially developed in relation to clinical practice from the 1980s. The idea behind this is that practitioners review evidence collected to make informed decisions about practice, which sounds an easy straightforward approach. However, the judgements made about evidence are crucial to ensuring this is a rigorous process and some general pointers for this were noted in Chapter 4. Building on this you could highlight the criteria that Pring and Thomas (2004) suggests are needed to judge evidence as shown in Table 6.2.

Table 6.2 What criteria can be employed to evaluate sources?

Criteria	Enabled by	Critical issues
Relevance	Establishing that the information constitutes information for (or against) some proposition	Does this sufficiently cover the quality of the evidence or the acknowledgement that there may be different perspectives on the proposition?
Sufficiency	Corroboration with other instances of the same kind of evidence or other kinds of evidence	Is this purely an issue of quantity? How much evidence is sufficient?
Veracity	Establishes that the process of collecting the evidence has been free from distortion and as far as possible uncontaminated by vested interests	Is it always possible to find out about the funding of evidence collected? How might I know about the influences on the evidence collection?

Adapted from Pring and Thomas (2004, p 5).

One essential factor to consider is how the evidence is collected in the first place? Slavin (2002) suggests that the '*gold standard*' in relation to the collection of evidence is through randomised controlled trials (RCT) and he argues that any other methods of evidence are less robust. Slavin appears to argue that there is a difference between evidence collected from research, ideally only using RCTs and evidence from personal experience or observation, which creates a hierarchy in relation to trust and reliability of the evidence collected. RCTs involve participants being randomly assigned to groups and then one of the groups is identified as a control group, which has no intervention or treatment and the other groups receive the intervention but not necessarily all in the same way and then results from all groups are compared against the control group.

For practitioners, however, RCTs are not the most appropriate methods of collecting evidence to inform practice as they bring with them critical issues of equity, equal opportunities and ethics in the workplace. What, for example, happens to children assigned to a control group? Are they accessing the same opportunities as those in any intervention group? In contrast research and evaluation that focuses on noticing what is occurring in practice and collating the evidence in order to change practice does provide a rationale for reviewing evidence. The idea is to become more aware of noticing specific events, incidents or other phenomena that occur, why you have noticed this specific thing and how you respond.

Noticing

Once you begin to notice specific things, you give these your more focused attention, selecting what you pay attention to and what you do not. Mason (2002) uses an example from his own practice. He noticed that he was repeating student's words back to them and this had become a habit. From his awareness of this practice he then did not make a value judgement about whether this was good or bad but began to notice the choices he made about whether or not to use this strategy in his teaching. This process sounds easy but it does take practice to begin to really notice things in practice. It can be a skill that could be practised with students observing the same clip of practice and discussing what they noticed. As they observe practice, this strategy enables the observer to pay attention to things they might not previously have noticed. This elaborated notion of noticing is depicted in Figure 6.1.

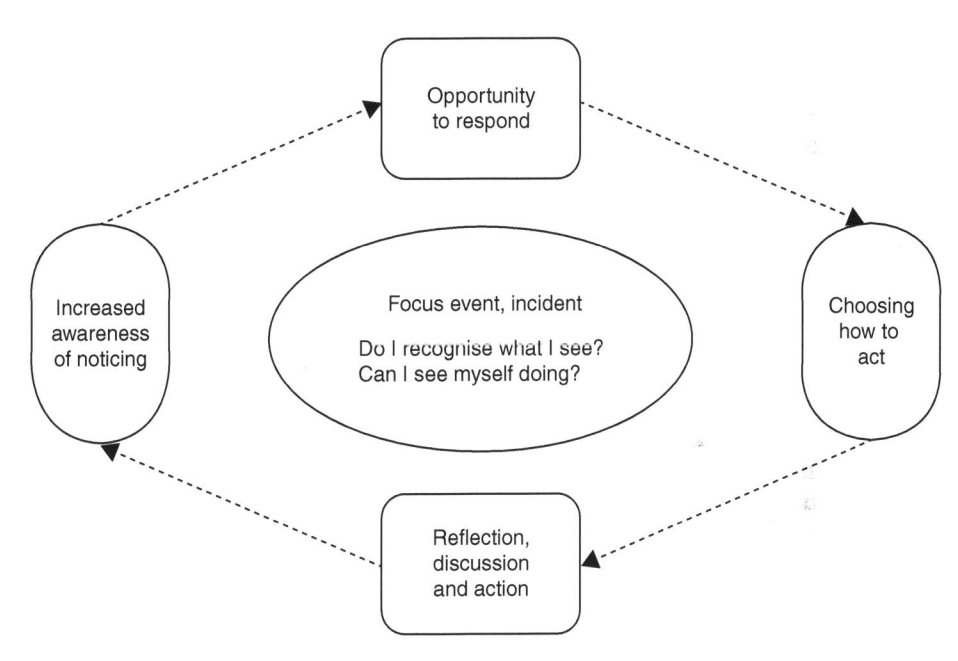

Figure 6.1 The process of 'noticing'.

Adapted from: Supporting ITE students in becoming reflective teachers. A set of discussion activities for ITE early years educators – activity sheet 1 (NCTEM). (www.ncetm.org.uk/public/files/6504301/activity+sheet+1.pdf)

Reflection

» Do you have a specific strategy in your teaching of students that has become a habit?

» Are you able to notice yourself using this strategy, just as Mason did?

» As you become consciously aware of the use of the strategy can you make choices about how you could respond differently?

» How might you argue against the ideas that RCT is the best way to ensure rigour in evidence collection?

Questioning *rule-bound* behaviours

Rules, in terms of human behaviour, form the boundary between what is acceptable or not. The boundaries of the rules are in most cases determined by a selected group/individual who have the power to both create the rules and to enforce them. These can be rules that are part of procedures and practices that are agreed by all and these become '*formal rules*'. The ideas about rule-bound behaviour are associated with principal–agent theory developed in the field of economics but are now more widely applied to organisational management and behaviour.

The principal designs the rules of a game that is going to be played over time by the agent and sticks to these rules no matter what happens during the relationship.

(Laffont and Martimort, 2002, p 290)

In organisations the agent is the person in the managing role. In large organisations rules are often in place to ensure consistency of approach and can focus on specific ways of doing things. Any induction process will in part be about helping anyone new to the organisation to understand the contextual rules and to make sense of their role within the organisation and the specific sets of roles associated with their role or position.

In all organisations there are also '*informal rules*' that become practice over time and are usually linked to statements such as '*We always do it like this*'. For the individual new to an organisation these can be more difficult to access and their status as rules can be unclear. Are they actually rules or have they become custom and practice over time? As practitioners we respond to rules in a number of ways, one of which can be an emotional level on which we feel that the imposition of rules is an attack on our personal and professional freedoms or autonomy.

Students often require guidance about how to navigate the layers of management in larger organisations from a '*room leader*' to a nursery headteacher as both layers assume formal and informal rules are understood by all staff working in the setting. You will need to explore this with students prior to any placement and how to handle any misconceptions around actual rules.

Part of developing the informed practitioner view is questioning the rule-bound behaviours within any organisation.

Reflection

» Consider in your role the formal rules that exist in your organisation that may relate to course design and content and possibly to the quality assurance process.

» Having considered these, think about how possible conflicts arise and are resolved.

» Consider the informal rules that have become custom and practice for either yourself or for your work with the students.

» How will you get your students to question rule-bound behaviours they observe particularly in practice?

Understanding the perspective of practitioners from other disciplines

When your students are in early years settings they will potentially be working alongside people in different professional roles including social workers, teachers, teaching assistants, speech therapists, health visitors and others. Each one of these professionals will have a perspective on working with children and their families depending upon their role. Dahlberg et al describe the interconnections and tensions between theory and practice, as

a form of spiralling which allows for taking multiple perspectives, for looping between self-reflection and dialogue, for passing between the language of one's professional community (theories and practical wisdom) and one's personal passions, emotions, intuitions and experiences.

(Dahlberg et al, 1999, p 154)

Students need to be guided through the differing perspectives and how these will connect to their own roles in an early years setting. What can they learn from other professionals' expertise and where might tensions arise with competing agendas? Glenny and Roaf (2008) provided detailed research into multi-professional communication, recognising in the concluding chapter of their book that the relationships created in this way of working resulted in complex dynamics. Within a group of people from different professional backgrounds there can be competing agendas as each profession has slightly different values and ways of working and they may not share common ideals.

The relationships between professional groups can also vary depending upon the age of children that students are working with particularly on any placement. (You may find it helpful to link back to Chapter 4 on age-related practice.) Early years settings, for example, tend to have a flatter hierarchy than larger school environments. In the former a number of people might be expected to liaise with other professionals such as health visitors whilst in the latter there are often specific roles for liaison with outside agencies. This can create conflict between teams or individuals within the group. These will be important understandings requiring strong interpersonal skills to convey to students wishing to make a career in the early years and to prepare your students for potential leadership roles in the future. In the same way, understanding the perspective of parents and carers is discussed as part of developing professional practice in Chapter 5.

Communities of practice

One way of looking at building these relationships is to consider the notion of a community of practice. This situated learning perspective has been developed from an anthropological view of learning in specific contexts by Lave and Wenger (1991). Communities of practice are groups that come together regularly and learn collaboratively. There are three key elements of a community of practice: the domain, the community and the practice. The first is an indication of the connection between the members of the group, the second is the way in which members of the group interact and the third is the development of shared understandings, resources and ways of working together. The other ideas associated with communities of practice are '*legitimate peripheral participation*' and '*situated learning*'. In legitimate peripheral participation the members of the community move from the peripheral involvement to full participation as they develop their competences. Situated learning focuses on the contextualisation of knowledge and therefore new knowledge is constructed within the community of practice. This social theory of learning differs from other theoretical perspectives on learning as it '*placed learning in the context of our lived experiences of participation of the world*' (Wenger, 1998, p 3). Wenger goes on to expand on the key components of this social theory of learning, which are meaning, practice, community and identity. Meaning is how we talk about what we experience either individually or together as part of the community and how we make that learning meaningful. Practice is the discussion about our shared perspectives built up over time, which when linked to the available resources will support the communities' participation in activities. Community allows value to be assigned to specific activities and those who are engaged in the activities become competent. The final component is identity and this relates to the way in which learning changes individual identities and how this situates the individual in the community.

Guiding students into employment

Part of the success criteria of any programme is the employment after completion and educators have a role to play in assisting students through the recruitment process including application, references, mock interviews and handling feedback. You will have a role in helping students make the most of their practical experiences in any application. This will include completing forms, writing letters or compiling a CV. Part of the application process is establishing what kind of environment students want to work in, based upon their values and ideas about good practice. As a teacher educator you might discuss what to look for when visiting a potential place of work. What questions might they ask people already working there? This can be a greater challenge for students who have more limited practical experience and you may need to show them how knowledge and skills acquired elsewhere match person and/or role specifications when applying for jobs.

For students with a lot of existing or prior experience there are two areas of support we can offer as educators. The first involves general support about how we can help students to make best use of their experiences in the application process. The second is in how we can tailor course content or specific teaching sessions to address how we can best support trainees and already qualified professionals to be open to and to lead and manage change. In what ways can we provide more experienced students with opportunities to explore leadership roles through team working with fellow students, assignments or on placements as part of their training? This could be taking a lead on a presentation or organising a visit.

Networking

Networking is defined as the process of interacting with people to share information to develop professional and/or social contacts. This can be helpful to encourage among students in and across cohorts who can share information and support each other whilst studying. This can have a positive impact and can be facilitated through electronic and possibly through social media but it can also have some dangers. Zickuhr (2013) suggests that 85 per cent of people are online in some form of social media. However, Osman et al (2012) found that many people were not aware that the images or comments that they posted had an impact on their professional identity. Networks can be face-to-face and include visits to each other's workplaces, which can be a good source of professional dialogue and can assist reflection on their own practice. This can work well for both early years educators and students as it helps them keep in touch with what is going on across a wider range of settings. Donelan (2016) indicates how students use social media to obtain employment at the end of their studies. She also looked at how academic staff used social media to widen their networks and publicise their work outside their institutions. Blogging was a key activity identified in this small-scale qualitative study. The following are some suggestions about why and how you might use networking:

- *To gain information* – about recent/upcoming trends/events associated with the early years
- *To make contacts* – make contacts with others undertaking a similar role and to explore the possibility of discussion, visits etc
- *To connect* – connect with people in similar roles and this allows others to know about you
- *To obtain advice* – collect advice, tips, ways of working from others
- *To find solutions* – find solutions and help for your problems as others may well have encountered the same issues
- *To promote* – to promote yourself and your students within a professional community
- *To establish relationships* – establish and advance relations within your professional area to develop research and/or practice

It can be lonely if you are an early years educator on a programme on your own, so networking can be a good way of connecting with others. Here is one early years educator's view about networking at professional group meetings:

I find that I want to check things out with people doing similar roles as it helps my confidence. I am not the only one finding these issues with my students. I can share my ideas and pickup on other ways of doing things. This can be much better than a formal CPD session as it gives you more chance to talk and ask questions which are important to you and your context.

And then when considering students:

Two students who met and studied together on the Early Years Teacher programme established a strong link between their settings and have set up a social and professional network of the two staff groups which has included sharing events between the settings. This has not been something I have actively encouraged but been able to facilitate and now this has become self-sustaining.

Reflection

- Are you a member of any social media networks, such as Twitter, LinkedIn, Pinterest or Facebook? How have these helped you to develop your thinking and practice?
- Consider what you know about the networks your students have established, such as Facebook groups or WhatsApp chats. Are you involved in any of these networks?

- » What ethical considerations are required about the use of social media for teaching? And for professions? (You may find it useful to return to Chapter 3 where ethics is discussed in more detail.)
- » Have you discussed in teaching sessions how these could be used professionally rather than socially?
- » How might you encourage students to make use of existing networks and develop more contacts outside these? How do you offer advice on the appropriate use of professional vs private forums?

Mentoring and coaching

Mentoring and coaching is a key process to continue to develop your skills as a professional. A mentor is someone who is a more knowledgeable professional often as a result of greater experience who takes on the role of guiding and supporting another's professional development. You may well have had a mentor as part of your induction into the organisation in which you currently work. A mentor may also be someone who guides the novice through their practice in a specific context. Mentoring students means giving them support and ensuring that they build up their professional capacity, knowledge and skills and giving them feedback on their progress towards specific goals. The mentor will offer advice and possibly suggest actions in order to change practice, which is often directly linked to the mentor observing current practice.

Mentoring in the workplace often has a clear goal or outcome and can be linked to assessment of competences. The mentor's role is to give constructive feedback on performance. Constructive feedback should include specific information about performance both positive and negative, which is based upon observation and other relevant data such as plans. It should also include next steps in relation to progress in developing professional knowledge and skills. In many ways this can be likened to '*oral marking*'. Mixing the negative with positive can help the recipient hear what is said more easily, for example using a '*positive sandwich*': start with a positive, add the negative and end with how things might be altered.

Coaching is slightly different from mentoring as the coach does not have to have the professional knowledge of the person they are coaching. What is key is that a coach has the skills to ask appropriate questions of the person being coached (the client) in order that the client decides on their actions to reach their goals. The coach may give feedback on the client's actions or ways of thinking about things but does not offer advice or suggest specific courses of action. The most commonly used model applied to the coaching conversation is GROW, which structures the course of the conversation. The GROW model is often attributed to Sir John Whitmore (2010) from his work in the 1980s though a number of others also worked on its development including Graham Alexander and Alan Fine – all three are coaches within the business world. G stands for goals and this is about establishing what the client wants to get from the coaching sessions. R is for reality and this about exploring the context for the goals identified. O means an exploration of all the possible options available to the client in order to achieve the goals and can also be used to explore the potential obstacles or barriers to progress. Finally, W is the will or way forward identifying what the client will do to progress towards their goals. Some coaches use this to structure each conversation held with their client as it helps them manage the conversation but like all models this can be a '*limiter*' to the overall conversation. However, structure can assist a new coach as they develop their skills. In coaching conversations, the client is the one who owns the agenda and decides upon actions as this process is underpinned by the idea that the client is the expert on their own situation and has the ability to find their own solutions. The coach's role is to help the client find those answers through the use of questioning and reflecting back to the client what is observed and heard.

Both mentors and coaches should have at the very least basic training in the role and ideally undertake regular continuing professional development and supervision associated with their role as a support for the mentors and coaches and their clients. Both processes should also have an agreed contract, which establishes the ground rules for the relationships including issues around confidentiality, frequency and length of meetings and an understanding of the roles and responsibilities.

Reflection

» For your own development consider whether a mentor or a coach would be the most appropriate as a support for your own development.

» Consider the kind of conversations you have with your students. Are they more mentoring or coaching?

» How will you support those you train to develop their mentoring and coaching role?

Continuing professional development (CPD) outside and inside your organisation

As an educator you will be involved in thinking about the professional development of your students but it is essential, too, to consider your own professional development. You might be seeking general teaching development but also subject specific development opportunities, depending upon your own background and route into working in higher education. For example, you might have a lot of practical experience of working with young children and colleagues in settings but more limited experience of working in higher education.

Reflection

One early years educator found the transition to working in higher education a challenge.

I came with lots of experience of working in settings with children, their families and the staff in settings but this didn't prepare me for working with students in college. I felt pulled in different directions. I knew students needed both practical tips but also the underpinning theories but getting this across in sessions was easier said than done. I wasn't prepared for the students' level of challenge around the content of sessions.

You may read the educator's comments above and feel a resonance with their thoughts as you developed into the role of an early years educator. Alternatively, you may have had different experiences as you made the transition from practitioner to educator. Consider what were the biggest challenges for you in making that transition and how did you overcome these?

Continuing professional development (CPD) can cover a wide range of activities though most people's first thought is about courses that focus on knowledge and skill development. These may or may not be accredited programmes. Many activities will take place inside institutions that are part of the day-to-day business but do have elements of CPD from formal course reviews, which feed into alterations for the following year to informal conversations with colleagues. (Informal conversations are also mentioned in Chapter 2.) CPD can also encompass simply reading and reflecting on practice either by yourself or with others. Additionally, CPD may include external conferences and networking (as previously explored) and social media. External professional development can be especially useful to assist in networking in relation to your specialist areas.

More formally, Beckingham and Nerantzi (2015) note that:

Teaching in HE in the UK has been professionalised in recent years (Dearing Report, 1997; DfES, 2003; Browne Report, 2010), and it is recognised that the initial and continuous professional development of teachers in HE and others who support learning has a significant impact on the quality of teaching and the student experience (BIS, 2011).

(Beckingham and Nerabntzi, 2015, p 109)

In reviewing this trajectory towards a professional and qualified staff in higher education they also noted that there are a number of different organisations that CPD activities can be accessed through such as the Higher Education Academy now Advance HE, Joint Information Systems Committee (JISC), Staff and Educational Development Association (SEDA) and Association for Learning Technology (ALT). Many of these will involve some form of coaching or mentoring that can be helpful to signpost your own learning and will incidentally provide more opportunities for you to reflect on the professional development relationships you have with your own students.

> ### IN A **NUTSHELL**
>
> Being an informed practitioner is part of your professional identity and links with your values about early years practice. Understanding where specific policies and guidance come from and how you might begin to compare these with practice to make an *informed* decision about their inclusion in your curriculum and/or specific sessions for your students is a key part of developing their professional identity and ultimately in helping students into and within employment in the early years.

> ### REFLECTIONS ON **CRITICAL ISSUES**
>
> » This chapter has explored what it means to be an informed practitioner and why it is an important disposition to develop. Being an informed practitioner makes you a more effective early years educator. It has also explored how an early years educator can encourage students to become informed practitioners too. As an early years educator you have an ethical position as you serve as a role model for your students in demonstrating the process of continuous self-development, which in turns lends authenticity to your higher education teaching and feeds back positively at all levels of training. Professional dialogue is a key element in your own learning just as much as it is for those you support as students and developing professionals.

Further reading

Aubrey, K and Riley, A (2018) *Understanding and Using Challenging Educational Theories*. London: Sage.

Briggs, I and Briggs, M (2009) *Developing Early Years Leadership*. London: Continuum International Publishing Group.

Mason, J (2002) *Researching Your Own Practice: The Discipline of Noticing*. London: RoutledgeFalmer.

REFERENCES

Ainsworth, M D, Blehar, M C, Waters, E and Wall, S (1978) *Patterns of Attachment*. Hillsdale, NJ: Erlbaum.

Ang, L (2014) Rethinking the Role of Early Years Education. *Contemporary Issues in Early Childhood*, 15(2): 185–198.

Barron, I (2016) Flight Turbulence: The Stormy Professional Trajectory of Trainee Early Years Teachers in England. *International Journal of Early Years Education*, 24(3): 325–341.

Bassot, B (2013) *The Reflective Journal: Capturing Your Learning for Personal and Professional Development*. London: Palgrave Macmillan.

Beckingham, S and Nerantzi, C (2015) Scaling-up Open CPD for Teachers in Higher Education Using a Snowballing Approach. *Journal of Perspectives in Applied Academic Practices*, 3(1): 109–121.

BERA/TACTYC (2017) Early Childhood Research Review 2003–2017. [online] Available at: www.bera.ac.uk and www.tactyc.org.uk.

BIS (2011) *Students at the Heart of the System*. [online] Department for Business, Innovation & Skills, Norwich: TSO. Available at: www.gov.uk/government/uploads/system/uploads/attachment_data/file/31384/11-944-higher-education-students-at-heart-of-system.pdf.

Bleach, J (2013) Using Action Research to Support Quality Early Years Practice. *European Early Childhood Education Research Journal*, 21(3): 370–379.

Bolton, G (2010) *Reflective Practice: Writing and Professional Development*. London: Sage.

British Association of Early Childhood Education. [online] Available at: www.early-education.org.uk/ethics-principles.

Brock, A (2012) Building a Model of Early Years Professionalism from Practitioners' Perspectives. *Journal of Early Childhood Research*, 11(1): 27–44.

Bronfenbrenner, U (1979) *The Ecology of Human Development: Experimental by Nature and Design*. Cambridge, MA: Harvard University Press.

Brooker, L (2005) Learning to be a Child: Cultural Diversity and Early Years Ideology. In Yelland, N (ed) *Critical Issues in Early Childhood Education* (pp 131–145). Maidenhead: Open University Press.

Brooker, L (2010) Constructing the Triangle of Care: Power and Professionalism in Practitioner/Parent Relationships. *British Educational Research Journal*, 58(2): 181–196.

Brown, J and Isaacs, D (2005) *The World Cafe: Shaping our Futures Through Conversations That Matter*. San Francisco: Berrett-Koehler Publishers.

Browne Report (2010) *Securing a Sustainable Future for Higher Education*. Department for Employment and Learning. [online] Available at: www.delni.gov.uk/index/publications/pubs-higher-education/browne-report-student-fees.htm.

Brownhill, S and Oates, R (2017) Who Do You Want Me To Be? An Exploration of Female and Male Perceptions of 'Imposed' Gender Roles in the Early Years. *Education*, 45(5): 658–670.

Cagliari, P, Castagnetti, M, Giudici, C, Rinaldi, C, Vecchi, V and Moss, P (2016) Loris Malaguzzi and the Schools of Reggio Emilia: A Selection of His Writings and Speeches, 1945–1993. [online] Available at: www.taylorfrancis.com/books/9781317697060 (accessed 5 September 2018).

Campbell, E (2003) *The Ethical Teacher*. Maidenhead: Open University Press.

Carr, M and Lee, W (2012) *Learning Stories: Constructing Learner Identities in Early Education*. London: Sage.

Clarke, B and Younas, F (2017) 'Helping Parents to Parent', in London Social Mobility Commission.

REFERENCES

Cottle, M and Alexander, E (2012) Quality in Early Years Settings: Government, Research and Practitioners' Perspectives. *British Educational Research Journal*, 38(4): 635–654.

Cottle, M and Alexander, E (2014) Parent Partnerships and 'Quality' Early Years Services: Practitioners' Perspectives. *European Early Childhood Education Journal,* 22 (5): 637–659.

Cribb, A (2009) Professional Ethics: Whose Responsibility? In Gewirtz, S, Mahony, P, Hextall, I and Cribb, A (eds) *Changing Teacher Professionalism: International Trends, Challenges and Ways Forward* (pp. 31–42). London: Routledge.

Dahlberg, G, Moss, P and Pence, A (1999) *Beyond Quality in Early Childhood Education and Care: Postmodern Perspectives.* London: Falmer Press.

Dalli, C (2008) Pedagogy, Knowledge and Collaboration: Towards a Ground-up Perspective on Professionalism. *European Early Childhood Education Research Journal,* 16(2): 171–185. [online] Available at: www.tandfonline.com/doi/abs/10.1080/13502930802141600.

Dearing Report (1997*) Higher Education in the Learning Society.* [online] Department for Education and Employment. Available at: www.leeds.ac.uk/educol/ncihe.

Department for Education (2017) *Statutory Framework for the Early Years Foundation Stage, Setting the Standards for Learning, Development and Care for Children from Birth to Five.* London: Crown Publications.

Department of Health (2014) Australian Early Childhood Mental Health Initiative, *Connections with the National Quality Framework: Working with Parents and Carers*, Canberra: KidsMatter.

DfE (2017) *Early Years Foundation Stage Statutory Framework.* [online] Available at: www.gov.uk/government/publications/early-years-foundation-stage-framework--2.

DfES (2003) *The Future of Higher Education.* [online] Available at: www.bis.gov.uk/assets/BISCore/corporate/MigratedD/publications/F/future_of_he.pdf (accessed 1 February 2015).

DfES (2007) *The Early Years Foundation Stage: Setting the Standards for Learning, Development and Care for Children from Birth to Five,* London: DfES.

Donelan, H (2016) Social Media for Professional Development and Networking Opportunities in Academia. *Journal of Further and Higher Education,* 40(5): 706–729.

Drummond, M J (2012) *Assessing Children's Learning.* London: David Fulton.

Drury, R (2007) *Young Bilingual Learners at Home and at School: Researching Multilingual Voices.* Stoke-on-Trent: Trentham Books.

Dweck, C S (1999) *Self-theories: Their Role in Motivation, Personality and Development.* Philadelphia, PA: Psychology Press.

Dyer, M (2018) Being a Professional or Practising Professionally? *European Early Childhood Education Research Journal,* 26(3): 347–361.

Elfer, P (2012a) Emotion in Nursery Work: Work Discussion as a Model of Critical Professional Reflection. *Early Years,* 32(2): 129–141.

Elfer, P (2012b) *Key Persons in the Early Years: Building Relationships for Quality Provision in Early Years Settings and Primary Schools.* London: Routledge.

Elfer, P (2013) Key Persons in the Nursery: Building Relationships for Quality Provision. London: David Fulton Publishers.

Elfer, P (2015) Emotional Aspects of Nursery Policy and Practice: Progress and Prospect. *European Early Childhood Education Research Journal*, 23(4): 497–511.

REFERENCES

Elfer, P and Dearnley, K (2007) Nurseries and Emotional Well-being: Evaluating an Emotionally Containing Model of Professional Development. *Early Years,* 27(3): 267–279.

Epstein, J (2001) *School, Family and Community Partnerships.* New York: Westview Press.

Evangelou, M, Sylva, K, Edwards, A and Smith, T (2008) *Supporting Parents in Promoting Early Learning: The Evaluation of the Early Learning Partnership Project* (Research Report DCSF-RR039). London.

Evangelou, M and Wild, M (2014) Connecting Home and Educational Play: Interventions that Support Children's Learning. In Brooker, E, Blaise, M and Edwards, S (eds) *Sage Handbook of Play and Learning in Early Childhood* (pp 378–390). London: Sage.

Field, F (2010) *The Foundation Years: Preventing Poor Children Becoming Poor Adults.* The Report of the Independent Review on Poverty and Life Chances. Cabinet Office, London.

Fisher, J (2013) *Starting from the Child*, 4th edition. Maidenhead: Open University Press.

Fisher, J (2016) *Interacting or Interfering?* Maidenhead: Open University Press.

Fitzpatrick, A (2012) Working with Parents in Early Years Services. In Mhic Mhathúna, M and Taylor, M (eds) *Early Childhood Education and Care. An Introduction for Students in Ireland* (pp 262–274). Dublin: Gill and Macmillan.

Georgeson, J and Campbell-Barr, V (2015) Attitudes and the Early Years Workforce (Editorial). *Early Years,* 35(4): 321–332.

Gilson, C and Street, A (2013) Working Inclusively in the Early Years. In Wild, M and Street, A (eds) *Themes and Debates in Early Childhood Education* (pp 40–55). London: Learning Matters/Sage.

Glenny, G and Roaf, C (2008) *Multiprofessional Communication: Making Systems Work for Children.* Maidenhead: McGraw-Hill Education.

Haigh, N (2005) Everyday Conversation as a Context for Professional Learning and Development. *International Journal for Academic Development,* 10(1): 3–16.

Hallett, E (2013) We All Share a Common Vision and Passion: Early Years Professionals Reflect Upon Their Leadership of Practice Role. *Journal of Early Childhood Research,* 11(3): 312–325.

Henshall, A, Atkins, L, Bolan, R, Harrison, J and Munn, H (2018) 'Certified to Make a Difference': The Motivation and Perceptions of Newly Qualified Early Years Teachers in England. *Journal of Vocational Education & Training,* 1–19. [online] Available at: https://doi.org/10.1080/13636820.2018.1437063.

Howard, J (2010) Making the Most of Play in the Early Years: The Importance of Children's Perceptions. In Broadhead, P, Howard, J and Wood, E (eds) *Play and Learning in the Early Years* (pp 145–160). London: Sage Publications.

Hutchins, P (1972) *Titch.* London: Penguin.

Ingleby, E (2018) Early Years Educators' Perceptions of Professional Development in England: an Exploratory Study of Policy and Practice. *Professional Development in Education,* 44(1): 22–32.

Irvine, S and Price, J (2014) Professional Conversations: A Collaborative Approach to Support Policy Implementation, Professional Learning and Practice Change in ECEC. *Australasian Journal of Early Childhood,* 39(3): 85–93.

Janmaat, J G (2018) Educational Influences on Young People's Support for Fundamental British Values. *British Educational Research Journal,* 44(2): 251–273.

Keys Adair, J and Doucet, F (2014) The Impact of Race and Culture on Play in Early Childhood Classrooms, in Brooker, E, Blaise, M and Edwards, S (eds) *Sage Handbook of Play and Learning in Early Childhood* (pp 359–365). London: Sage.

REFERENCES

Knopf, H and Swick K (2007) How Parents Feel About Their Child's Teacher/School: Implications for Early Childhood Professionals. *Early Childhood Education Journal*, 34(4): 291–296.

Knowles, G and Holmstrom, R (2013) *Understanding Family Diversity and Home-School Relations: A Guide for Students and Practitioners in Early Years and Primary Settings*. London: Routledge.

Kwon, Y-I (2002) Changing Curriculum for Early Childhood Education in England. *Early Childhood Research and Practice*, 4 (2) 2–13.

Laffont, J J and Martimort, D (2002) *The Theory of Incentives: The Principal–Agent Model*. Princeton, PA: Princeton University Press.

Lave, J and Wenger, E (1991) *Situated Learning. Legitimate Peripheral Participation*. Cambridge: Cambridge University Press.

Lightfoot, S and Frost, D (2015) The Professional Identity of Early Years Educators in England: Implications for a Transformative Approach to Continuing Professional Development. *Professional Development in Education*, 41(2): 401–418.

Lunn Brownlee, J, Scholes, L, Walker, S and Johansson, E (2016) Critical Values Education in the Early Years: Alignment of Teachers' Personal Epistemologies and Practices for Active Citizenship. *Teaching and Teacher Education*, 59: 261–227.

MacNaughton, G (2005) *Doing Foucault in Early Childhood Studies: Applying Poststructural Ideas*. London: Routledge.

MacNaughton, G and Hughes, P (2011) *Parents and Professionals in Early Childhood Settings*. Maidenhead: McGraw Hill.

Mason, J (2002) *Researching Your Own Practice: The Discipline of Noticing*. London: RoutledgeFalmer.

McMillan, M (1919) *The Nursery School*. London: J.M. Dent & Sons.

Members of the British Educational Research Association Early Years Special Interest Group (2002) *Early Years Research: Pedagogy, Curriculum and Adult Roles, Training and Professionalism*. [online] Available at: www.dpscitt.ac.uk/uploads/student_resources/beraearlyyearsreview31may03.pdf.

Molla, T and Nolan, A (2018) Identifying Professional Functionings of Early Childhood Educators. *Professional Development in Education*. DOI:10.1080/19415257.2018.1449006.

Morgan, R (2014) *The United Nations Convention on the Rights of the Child: How Children say the UK Is Doing*. [online] Ofsted. Available at: https://assets.publishing.service.gov.uk/government/uploads/system/uploads/attachment_data/file/379154/.

Moss, P (2014) *Transformative Change and Real Utopias in Early Childhood Education: A Story of Democracy, Experimentation and Potentiality*. London: Routledge.

Moss, P (2016) Why Can't We Get Beyond Quality? *Contemporary Issues in Early Childhood*, 17(1): 8–15.

Moyles, J (2001) Passion, Paradox and Professionalism in Early Years Education. *Early Years: An International Journal of Research and Development*, 21(2): 81–95.

Murray, J, McDowall Clark, R (2013) Reframing Leadership as a Participative Pedagogy: The Working Theories of Early Years Professionals *Early Years: An International Journal of Research and Development*, 33(3): 289–301.

Neaum, S (2016) School Readiness and Pedagogies of Competence and Performance: Theorising the Troubled Relationship between Early Years and Early Years Policy. *Early Years*, 24(3): 239–253.

ONS (2018) Statistical Bulletin. Families and Households: 2017. Office of National Statistics. [online] Available at: www.ons.gov.uk/peoplepopulationandcommunity/birthsdeathsandmarriages/families/bulletins/familiesandhouseholds/2017 (accessed 12 June 2018).

REFERENCES

Osgood, J (2006) Deconstructing Professionalism in Early Childhood Education: Resisting the Regulatory Gaze. *Contemporary Issues in Early Childhood*, 7(1): 5–14.

Osgood, J (2010) Reconstructing Professionalism in ECEC: The Case for the 'Critically Reflective Emotional Professional'. *Early Years*, 30(2): 119–133.

Osman, A, Wardle, A and Caesar, R (2012) Online Professionalism and Facebook Falling Through the Generation Gap. *Medical Teacher*, 34(8): e549–e556. DOI:10.3109/0142159X.2012.668624

Page, J and Elfer, P (2013) The Emotional Complexity of Attachment Interactions in Nursery. *European Early Childhood Education Research Journal*, 21(4): 553–567. DOI: 10.1080/1350293X.2013.766032.

Pring, R and Thomas, G (eds) (2004) *Evidence-Based Practice in Education*. Maidenhead: Open University Press.

QAA (2014) *Subject Benchmarks: Early Childhood Studies*. [online] Available at: www.qaa.ac.uk/en/Publications/Documents/SBS-early-childhood-studies-14.pdf (accessed 16 June 2018).

QCA (2000) *Curriculum Guidance for the Foundation Stage*, Sudbury: Qualifications and Curriculum Authority.

Rayner, S (2014) Playing by the Rules? The Professional Values of Head Teachers Tested by the Changing Policy Context. *Management in Education*, 28(2): 38–43.

Reynolds, A and Clements, M (2005) Parental Involvement and Children's School Success. In Patrikakou, E, Weisberg, R, Redding, S and Walberg, H (eds) *School-Family Partnerships for Children's Success* (pp 109–130). New York: Teachers College Press.

Roberts-Holmes, G P (2015) The Datafication of Early Years Pedagogy: 'If the Teaching Is Good, Then Data Should Be Good and If There Is Bad Teaching, There Is Bad Data'. *Journal of Education Policy*, 30(3): 302–315. DOI: 10.1080/02680939.2014.924561.

Roberts-Holmes, G and Bradbury, A (2016) Governance, Accountability and the Datafication of Early Years Education in England. *British Educational Research Journal*, 42(4): 600–613.

Roberts-Holmes, G and Bradbury, A (2017) Primary Schools and Network Governance: A Policy Analysis of Reception Baseline Assessment. *British Educational Research Journal*, 43(4): 671–682.

Robson, J (2017) *Fundamental British Values in Early Childhood Education and Care: Practitioners' and Children's Navigation of the Ideology in Practice*. Paper presented to British Curriculum Forum, British Educational Research Association, London, June 2017.

Rogers, C (2002) Defining Reflection: Another Look at John Dewey and Reflective Thinking. *Teachers College Record*, 104(4): 842–866.

Salzberger-Wittenberg, I, Williams G and Osbourne E (1983) *The Emotional Experience of Learning and Teaching*. London: Routledge and Kegan Paul.

Sameroff, A J (2009) *The Transactional Model of Development: How Children and Contexts Shape Each Other*. Washington, DC: American Psychological Association.

Sammons, P, Sylva, K, Melhuish, E, Siraj-Blatchford, I, Taggart, B, Barreau, S and Grabbe, Y (2008) *The Influence of School and Teaching quality in Children's progress in primary school. Effective Pre-school and Primary Education 3–11 (EPPE 3–11)*. London: Institute of Education, University of London/DCSF.

Sammons, P, Sylva, K, Melhuish, E, Siraj-Blatchford, I, Taggart, B and Hunt, S (2008) *Influences on Children's Attainment and Progress in Key Stage 2: Cognitive Outcomes in Year 6. DCSF Research Report DCSF-RR048*. London.

Sant, E and Hanley, C (2018) Political Assumptions Underlying Pedagogies of National Education: The Case of Student Teachers Teaching 'British Values' in England. *British Educational Research Journal*, 44(2): 319–337.

REFERENCES

SCAA (1996) *Desirable Outcomes for Children's Learning on Entering Compulsory Education.* Crown copyright.

Senge, P (1994) *The Fifth Discipline Fieldbook: Strategies and Tools for Building a Learning Organization.* London: Nicolas Brearley Publishing.

Silberfeld, C and Mitchell, H (2018) Graduates' Perspectives on Their Early Childhood Studies Degrees. *Early Years.*

Siraj-Blatchford, I (2009) Conceptualising Progression in the Pedagogy of Play and Sustained Shared Thinking in Early Childhood Education: A Vygotskian perspective. *Educational and Child Psychology.* 26(2): 1–15.

Slavin, R E (2002) Evidence-Based Education Policies: Transforming Educational Practice and Research. *Educational Researcher,* 31(7): 15–21.

Smilansky, S (1968) *The Effects of Sociodramatic Play on Disadvantaged Preschool Children.* New York: John Wiley & Sons.

Soni, A (2018) Opportunities for Development: the Practice of Supervision in Early Years Provision in England. *International Journal of Early Years Education.* DOI:10.1080/09669760.2018.1444586.

Stanfield, R D (ed) (2000) *The Art of Focused Conversation: 100 Ways to Access Group Wisdom in the Workplace.* Toronto: Canadian Institute of Cultural Affairs.

Street, A and Wild, M (2013) Working with Families in the Early Years. In Wild, M and Street, A (eds) *Themes and Debates in Early Childhood* (pp 109–125). London: Sage/Learning Matters.

Sylva, K, Melhuish, E, Sammons, P, Siraj-Blatchford, I and Taggart, B (2004) *The Effective Provision of Pre-School Education (EPPE) Project: Findings from Pre-School to the End of Key Stage 1,* Sure Start, IoE. [online] Available at: www.ioe.ac.uk/projects.

Sylva, K, Melhuish, E, Sammons, P, Siraj-Blatchford, I and Taggart, B (2010) *Early Childhood Matters. Evidence from the Effective Pre-school and Primary Education Project.* London. Routledge.

Taggart, G (2011) Don't We Care?: The Ethical Emotional Labour of Early Years Professionalism. *Early Years,* 31(1): 85–95.

Taggart, G (2014) Compassionate Pedagogy: the Ethics of Care in Early Childhood Professionalism. *European Early Childhood Research Journal,* 24(2): 173–185.

Taggart, G (2015) Sustaining Care: Cultivating Mindful Practice in Early Years Professional Development. *Early Years,* 35(4): 381–393.

Tan, S and Brown, J (2005) The World Café in Singapore: Creating a Learning Culture through Dialogue. *The Journal of Applied Behavioural Science,* 41(1): 83–90.

Tanner, E, Welsh, E and Lewis, J (2006) The Quality-defining Process in Early Years Services: A Case Study. *Children and Society,* 20(1): 4–16.

Tickell, C (2011) *The Early Years: Foundations for Life, Health and Learning – An Independent Report on the Early Years Foundation Stage to Her Majesty's Government.* [online] Available at: https://assets.publishing.service.gov.uk/government/uploads/system/uploads/attachment_data/file/180919/DFE-00177-2011.pdf.

Urban, M (2015) From 'Closing the Gap' to an Ethics of Affirmation. Reconceptualising the Role of Early Childhood Services in Times of Uncertainty. *European Journal of Education,* 50(3): 293–306.

Urban, M, Vandenbroeck, M, Van Leare, K, Lazzari, A and Peeters, J (2012) Towards Competent Systems in Early Childhood Education and Care. Implications for Policy and Practice. *European Journal of Education,* 47(4): 508–526.

REFERENCES

Vandenbroeck, M (2009) Let Us Disagree. *European Early Childhood Education Journal,* 17(2): 165–170.

Vincent, C and Braun, A (2011) 'I Think a Lot of It Is Common Sense…': Early Years Students, Professionalism and the Development of a 'Vocational Habitus'. *Journal of Education Policy,* 26(6): 771–785.

Ward, U (2018) How Do Early Childhood Practitioners Define Professionalism in Their Interaction with Parents? *European Early Childhood Education Research Journal,* 26(2): 274–284.

Wenger, E (1998) *Communities of Practice: Learning Meaning and Identity.* Cambridge: Cambridge University Press.

Whitmore, J (2010) *Coaching for Performance: GROWing Human Potential and Purpose: The Principles and Practice of Coaching and Leadership.* London: Nicholas Brearley Publishing.

Wood, E (2010) Developing Integrated Pedagogical Approaches to Play and Learning. In Broadhead, P, Howards, J and Wood, E (eds) *Play and Learning in the Early Years* (pp 9–26). London: Sage.

Yelland, N (2005) *Critical Issues in Early Childhood Education.* Maidenhead: Open University Press.

Youell, B (2006) *The Learning Relationship: Psychoanalytic Thinking in Education.* London: Karnac.

Zeldin, T (1998) *Conversation: How Talk Can Change Our Lives.* London: Harvill.

Zickuhr, K (2013) *Who's Not Online and Why.* PEW Internet Research. [online] Available at: www.pewinternet.org/2013/09/25/whos-not-online-and-why.

INDEX

A

adult, role in child-initiated collaborative activities, 40–41
Alexander, E, 53
Alexander, Graham, 77
attitudes
    description of, 25–26
    and dialogue, 18
    towards language, 60
    to play, 59
    and reflection, 21
Australia
    Department of Health's recommendation for fathers' engagement, 47

B

Barron, I, 7–8
baseline assessment, 50, 55, *see also* children's learning assessment
Bassot, B, 19
Beckingham, S, 79
'being a professional' versus 'practising professionally', 3
beliefs, 14, 26, 27–28, 31, 36
    and curriculum, 32–33
    and policy, 30
    and practice, 32–33
bi-directional approach, 62
bilingual learners, 60
Birth to Three curriculum, 32
Bleach, J, 14–15, 22
Bolton, G, 19, 21
Braun, A, 5
British Association of Early Childhood Education, 28
British Education Research Association (BERA), 2
Britishness, interpretations of, 29–30
Brock, A, 9
Bronfenbrenner, U, 39
Brooker, L, 54, 56, 59–60
Brownhill, S, 4
Bruce, Tina, 31

C

Caesar, R, 75
Campbell, E, 27
Campbell-Barr, V, 5, 26
child-initiated collaborative activities, adult's role in, 40–41
children's learning assessment, *see* baseline assessment
    learning stories, 44–46
    observations, 44
    standardised testing, 43–44
children's play, *see* child-initiated collaborative activities, adult's role in
Clarke, B, 60
Clements, M, 46
coaching, 77–78, *see also* mentoring
co-construction, 38
Cohen-Emerique, M, 59
colleagues, conversations with, *see* conversations, with colleagues
communities, 7, 54, 62
    constructive working with, 60–63
communities of practice, 74
compassionate leadership, 34–35
    supporting students to recognise compassion, 35–36
conflicting standpoints, 36–37
constructive feedback, 77
continuing professional development (CPD) programme, 14–15
continuous professional development (CPD) programme, 74
conversations, 14, *see also* professional dialogue
    with colleagues, 18, 19
    about ideas, 18
    and professional identity development, 14–15
    protocols, 18
    unfettered conversation, 18
Cottle, M, 53
Cribb, A, 27
critical thinking, 51
cultural dissonance, 59
culture and context for early learning, 25
culture shock, 59
curriculum
    and beliefs, 32–33
    documentation, 28
Curriculum Guidance, 28

D

Dahlberg, G, 73
Dalli, C, 14
datafication, 55
Desirable Learning Outcomes (DLOs), 28
Dewey, John, 20, 21, 27
dialogism, 7
dialogue, *see* professional dialogue
dispositions, 5, 25–26
Donelan, H, 75
Drury, R, 60

Dweck, C S, 42
Dyer, M, 3

E

Early Years Foundation Stage (EYFS), 27, 28, 45
Early Years Teacher, 2, 34
educational play, 59
educators, definition of, 1
Effective Provision of Pre-school /Primary and Secondary Education (EPPSE) project, 6
Elfer, Peter, 8, 9, 34, 57
emotional labour, 8–9, 48
environotype children, 38–39
Epstein, J, 47
ethics, 26, 27
  of care, 5, 6, 35
  personal and professional ethics, difference between, 27
  and policy, 30
Evangelou, M, 62
evidence-based practice (EBP), 51, 69–70
  noticing, 71–72
extrinsic motivation, 42

F

families, 7, *see also* parental engagement; parents
  constructive working with, 60–63
  as cultural context for learning, 57–58
  definitions of, 53–54
  diversity in, 57–58
  and professionals relationship, 53–55
Fine, Alan, 77
Fisher, J, 25, 42
Foundation Stage Profile, 55
France, educational play in, 59
Froebel, Friedrich, 31
fundamental British values (FBV), 29–30

G

gender, in workforce, 4
Georgeson, J, 5, 26
Glenny, G, 73
GROW model of coaching, 77–78
guiding students into employment, 73–74
  networking, 75–77

H

Haigh, N, 18
Hanley, C, 29
Henshall, A, 2
Hochschild, Arlie, 8
Holmstrom, R, 57

Howard, J, 40, 41
Hutchins, Pat, 32

I

informal rules, 72, 73
informed practitioner, 65–66
  aspects of, 66–69
  continuous professional development (CPD), 74
  early years educator as, 69
  evidence-based practice (EBP), 69–70
  guiding students into employment, 73–74
  questioning rule bound behaviours, 72–73
  student as, 66–68
  student as, early years educators' role in, 69
  understanding different professional roles, 73–74
interaction, and learning, 38, *see also* professional dialogue
intercultural dialogue, 59, 60
intrinsic motivation, 42
Irvine, S, 15
Isaacs, Susan, 31

J

Janmaat, J G, 30

K

Katz, Lilian, 26
key person system, 48–49, 57
Keys Adair, J, 59
Knowles, G, 57
Kwan, Y-I, 31

L

language constraints, 60
Lave, J, 74
leadership, 69, 74, 75
  compassionate leadership, 34–35
  and ethics, 27
learning environments, 25, 34, 38
  at home, 46, 54, 56
  importance of, 28
  parent's contribution, 47
  and play, 40
  and real world settings, 42
  safe and supportive, 14
learning relationships
  baseline assessment, 50
  child's interests and experiences, 42–43
  children as collaborators in, 40–42
  critical awareness and evidence-based approach development, 51
  definitions of, 38–39

learning relationships (*cont.*)
  development, influence of policy on, 49–50
  effectiveness assessment
    learning stories, 44–46
    observations, 44
    standardised testing, 43–44
  importance of care in, 48–49
  parental engagement, 46–48
  parents as key players, 46
learning stories, 44–46
legitimate peripheral participation, community of practice, 74

M

MacNaughton, G, 16
male students and employees, under-representation of, 4
Maslow's hierarchy of needs, 25
McDowall Clark, R, 34
McMillan, Margaret, 31
mentoring, 77, 78, *see also* coaching
mindfulness, 8
Molla, T, 9, 10
monologue, 18
Montessori, Maria, 31
Morgan, R, 34
Moss, Peter, 6, 73
motivation, influence on children, 42
Murray, J, 34

N

National Professional Qualification in Integrated Centre Leadership (NPQICL), 34
needs, hierarchy of, 25
Nerantzi, C, 79
networking, 75–77, 79
  social media, 75–76, 79
New Zealand, 33, 62
Nolan, A, 9, 10
noticing, 45, 70, 71–72

O

Oates, R, 4
Open Air Nursery, 31
Osgood, J, 5
Osman, A, 75

P

Page, J, 34
parental engagement, 46, *see also* families
  Epstein's model, 47
  promotion and facilitation of, 47–48
  socioeconomic factors, 46
  time constraints, 46
parents, 54, *see also* families
  as deficient educators, 55–57
  as first educators, 55–57
  empowerment, 60
  involvement, *see* parental engagement
  positive skills development, 60
peer play, 40
Pen Green Children's Centre, 56
personal and professional ethics, difference between, 27
phenotype children, 38
philosophies, 7, 26, 28, 31–32
  beliefs and practice, 32–33
physical development workshop, 39
play-based learning, 31, 40–41
policy development, 2–3
positive dissensus, 16, 17
positive relationships, 14, 17, 32–33, 53, 54, 57
Price, J, 15
professional continuities, 3
professional conversations, *see* conversations; professional dialogue
professional development domains, 10
professional dialogue, 8, 13, 62, *see also* conversations
  conversations with colleagues, 18
  definition of, 14
  and evidence-based approach, 51
  in groups, 22
  and learning relationship, 49
  and professional identity development, 14–15
  and quality in the early years, 16–17
  reflecting together, 22–23
  reflective writing, 19–22
  usefulness, 17
professional ethics, *see* ethics
professional identity, 28
  definition of, 14
  development, and dialogue, 14–15
  and reflecting together, 22
professional training, 2
professionalism, 62
  typology of, 9
professionals, definition of, 1

Q

qualifications, 2, 3, 6
quality in the early years
  and competences, 6–8
  minimum quality provision, 16
  and professional dialogue, 16–17
  and values, 16

R

randomised controlled trials (RCTs), 70
Rayner, S, 30

reflective journal, 19, 26
   analyse the account, 19
reflective writing, 19–20
   example, 20–21
   manage the moral and ethical dimensions, 21
   risk in, 21–22
   and shared learning, 15
Reggio Emilia approach to learning, 32, 33
regulation of early education and care, 49–50
relationships
   importance of, 28
   learning, *see* learning relationships
   positive relationships, 14, 17, 32–33, 53, 54, 57
   between professional groups, 74
religious beliefs, and cultural practices, 59
Reynolds, A, 46
Roaf, C, 73
Roberts-Holmes, G, 55
Robson, J, 30
Rogers, Carol, 20
rule bound behaviours, 72–73

S

Sameroff, A J, 38
Sant, E, 29
Scandinavian models, 33
school failure, 55
Senge, P, 18
Siraj-Blatchford, I, 40
situated learning, community of practice, 74
Slavin, R E, 70
small group instruction, student/trainee's role in, 41–42
Smilansky, S, 40–41
social media, 75–76, 79, *see also* networking
socio-dramatic play, 41
Soni, A, 6
Street, A, 54
students
   definition of, 1
   knowing about, 4–6
   role as direct instructors in small groups, 41–42
   role in child-initiated collaborative activities, 40–41
supervision of practice, 6
Sylva, K, 33

T

TACTYC, 2
Taggart, G, 8, 27, 34
Tanner, E, 16

Te Whariki (New Zealand Early years' curriculum), 33, 62
Thomas, G, 69
Tickell, Dame Clare, 28
Titch (Hutchins), 32
trainees
   role as direct instructors in small groups, 41–42
   role in child-initiated collaborative activities, 40–41
transaction, and learning, 38

U

unfettered conversation, 18
United Nations Convention on Human Rights, 34
Urban, M, 7

V

values, 14, 16, 17, 22, 26, 27–28, 31, 36
   definition of, 27
   fundamental British values, 29–30
   and policy, 30
Vandenbroeck, M, 57–58
Vincent, C, 5
Vygotsky, L, 38

W

Ward, U, 46
Wardle, A, 75
Wenger, E, 74
Whitmore, Sir John, 77
Wild, M, 54, 62
work discussion approach, to emotional responses, 9, *see also* conversations; professional dialogue
work-play dichotomies, 41
workshops, 41
writing, reflective, *see* reflective writing

Y

Youell, B, 54
Younas, F, 60

Z

Zeldin, Theodore, 18
Zickuhr, K, 75